10157

792.8 Streatfeild, Noel
S

A young person's
guide to ballet

MAR 9	DATE		
		NOV 10	
JAN 17			
NOV 2		XXX	
	NOV 10		
JAN 8			
SEP 29 80			
OCT 1 9 1981			
FEB 4 1984			
MAR 2 6 1984			

792.8   10157
S

Streatfeild

A young person's guide
to ballet

WITHDRAWN

p. 16

p. 80

1

2

3

p. 23

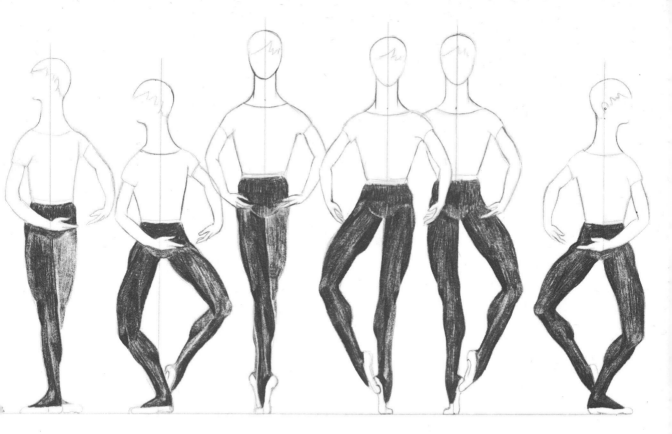

p. 38

B

A

C

pp. 24–25

A YOUNG PERSON'S GUIDE TO BALLET

NOEL STREATFEILD

A YOUNG PERSON'S GUIDE TO BALLET

Drawings by Georgette Bordier

FREDERICK WARNE & CO LTD
FREDERICK WARNE & CO INC
LONDON : NEW YORK

10157

This illustrated edition copyright © 1975 The Felix Gluck Press Limited, Twickenham, England.
All rights reserved. No part of this publication may be reproduced, stored in a retrieval system or
transmitted in any form or by any means, electronic, mechanical, photocopying or otherwise, without
the prior permission of the publishers.

First published by Frederick Warne & Co. Ltd., London, England, 1975.

LIBRARY OF CONGRESS CATALOG CARD NO. 74-81666
ISBN 0 7232 1814 5

Filmset and printed in Great Britain by BAS Printers Limited, Wallop, Hampshire

Contents

Introduction

I cannot remember a time when I did not love watching people dance. When I was small the only dancing we had a chance to see was performed by amateurs. Star girl pupils of somebody's dancing class— boys never danced in those days. The girls danced what we called toe dancing, which meant on their pointes. I admired them enormously but I don't think I ever knew any of them personally. Our friends did what we did. That is to say, were sent once a week to a class, usually held in a friend's house. There we learnt exercises followed by Irish jigs, Scottish reels, scarf dances and, one term, a weird dance where we waved branches of dried palms. There was also a period when skirt dances were all the rage. For this dresses had to be what was called accordion pleated. We had to sit out the skirt dancing periods because our parents couldn't afford to buy us accordion pleated dresses. We had them in the end but by then the craze had died down and a Spanish phase had taken over. We had to have castanets for that period.

I do not now remember who took us to see the professional children dancers. They were called Lilah Field's Little Wonders. They danced in the theatre which was at the end of the pier. To us the children seemed geniuses and they probably were smart, cute and well trained, but what left me gasping was the leading ballerina. She was perhaps fourteen and danced, amongst other dances, THE DYING SWAN *which, though I did not know it, Pavlova had made famous. Her name was Ninette de Valois. She was, when she was older, to become a soloist with Diaghilev. She was also, with the aid of the great Lilian Baylis, to found the Vic-Wells ballet company, now called the Royal Ballet. For me she was a standard for my life of what great dancing ought to be. The dancers paid several visits to the south coast and somehow we girls (there were three of us) managed to see them. This was quite a feat for we had to pay for our seats ourselves, which must have meant much sacrifice when pocket money was three pennies a week.*

Boy on demi-pointe

10

When my father became Vicar of Eastbourne we went to a new school and there I found a little group of ballet lovers. Many of these were boarders whose homes were in London and they were able, in the holidays, to watch dancing when there was any. At that time there was no London ballet company and, though there were some good dancers, they danced mainly in music halls, to which children were not taken, and the dancers were again mainly girls; male dancers were still not taken seriously. However, this group of boarders had nearly all seen Pavlova dance and they collected picture postcards of her.

I have often wondered how those postcards brought Pavlova alive to me. I can see them still in my mind's eye: that magic and beauty of movement caught for ever on a piece of cardboard. I don't think I ever hoped to dance myself; that would have been plain idiotic for I was not even good at our simple dancing classes. What I did most passionately want was to watch great dancers to try and learn where their magic came from.

It was while I was living with the postcards of Pavlova that dancing fever hit our school. The Diaghilev company was coming to London and a party of girls from the school were to be taken to a matinée. There was a lot of talk about this great company but no clear statement. It seemed they were something quite new. That for those who saw them dance the world would never be the same again. But in answer to my endless questions I got very dull answers, which mostly boiled down to 'You must see them yourself.'

See them myself! How was I, with three pennies a week pocket money and parents, particularly my father, who actually disliked watching dancing, to get to London let alone buy a seat? So the school party went to London without me and I doubt if anybody knew that I felt as if my heart were bleeding because I was left behind.

It was all quite true. Most of that party which went from the school came back changed. In some ways they seemed stretched, as if they could see more than we who were left behind could see. Most of them struggled to pass on what they had seen. But who can pass on magic? In the end my persistence in asking what I daresay seemed silly questions was snubbed by the headmistress herself. She had been talking to a group of the girls who had been to see the ballet company, about colour. I forget now what she said but I know I burst in with 'What do they wear?' It was as if I had smudged a picture with dirty fingers. 'Really, Noel,' said my headmistress, 'if you can't ask sensible questions don't speak at all.'

Girl on full pointe

11

When I left school I went to the Academy of Dramatic Art to learn to be an actress. There, as one of the regular subjects, we learnt the rudiments of ballet. I adored the classes for they gave me a little insight into dancing mysteries. I knew in time about posture and turn-out and how a dancer breathes and counts. The master who taught us must have noticed how eagerly I snapped up any pearls of wisdom which fell from his lips, for he said one day: 'If I had been your dancing master ten years ago I would have made a dancer out of you.' It was not true, I was much too tall so I would have got nowhere. My place in life was to be a devoted viewer, and that I have always been.

Fate took me right away from ballet companies for some years. When at last I came back to London I discovered the Vic-Wells ballet. In those days it was possible to get wonderfully cheap theatre seats and I spent almost all I had on them. I saw Markova and Anton Dolin and got to know every soloist by sight and by name. Amongst these was the little Margot Fonteyn, already being groomed for stardom. Those were wonderful days for there was such pride and hope in the theatre; it seemed to me impossible to believe that all this beauty was born from the energy, executive ability and imagination of the fourteen-year-old Ninette de Valois I had seen dancing on the pier at St Leonards-on-Sea.

At the same time a new ballet company came to Covent Garden. It was called the de Basil Company or the Ballet Russe de Monte Carlo. In the company were three children, daughters of Russian refugees, who had learnt to dance from Russian émigré teachers in Paris. Their names were Toumanova, Baronova and Riabouchinska. It was from this company, and especially from Baronova, that I learnt what perfection in dancing is. It is a moment when everything is at the point of ecstasy at the same instant. To give this the dancer has to be exceptionally musical which Baronova is. The moment—and I can still catch it in my memory—came in the ballet called LES PRÉSAGES *danced to Tchaikovsky's fifth symphony. Baronova wore a crimson tunic and it was her entrance with her lover—danced by David Lichine—that gave me my great moment. I saw that ballet several times and never once did that breath-catching entrance fail to lift me almost into another world. Since then I have collected many such moments from, amongst others, Margot Fonteyn, Nureyev and Ulanova; they may not come often, but to the ballet lover they are worth waiting for.*

Being an actress in those days I went where there was work. It was a pantomime which produced my next dancers and these I got to know.

12

For the pantomime played for about three months and every opportunity I got I studied our troupe of child dancers. Many of the children were brilliant both as actors and dancers, but what I found enthralling was their training. Like most stage children they were highly disciplined. They came in most cases from very poor homes but, once they joined the troupe, they were educated to live in comfort. I often wondered how their mothers managed when they came home between jobs. To them such things as dressing-gowns, bedroom slippers and even tooth brushes were unbelievable luxuries. Did these mothers accept that such things were necessary for a child dancer? When, about three years later, I gave up acting and became a writer, I found my careful though, at the time, purposeless study of those children invaluable. Do you wonder that I wrote a book called BALLET SHOES?

It is because being a ballet lover has given me a lifetime of matinées and evenings of rapture that I agreed to write this book.

I know every library is bursting with books often by famous dancers, but I wanted a book for ordinary children such as I was. Longing to watch, to know and even to feel what it is like to be a dancer.

It is not I think possible to write a book about how to watch ballet—so much depends on where you live. So I have made up two children, Anna and Peter, who learn to dance and, at the same time, pick up a little ballet history. What this book tries to tell you is that, quite apart from a career, dancing is a lovely thing to be able to do and, because you have learnt something about it, watching dancing will give you pleasure all your life.

Noel Streatfeild

CHAPTER ONE

Anna and Peter

This is the story of a boy and a girl who want to learn to dance. Their names are Anna and Peter. The dancing teacher their parents have found is called Miss Deen.

Miss Deen, when a child, was trained to dance by an aunt who had been a ballet dancer. The aunt had danced round the world with Pavlova. It had been planned that when Miss Deen was fifteen she would try to get an audition for the senior ballet school belonging to the Royal Ballet. But fate was against her, she contracted rheumatic fever which left her with a weak heart. For one year after she recovered she was not allowed to dance at all, then only for a short while each day. In the end, when she was entirely recovered, it was decided she was too behind in her training to be a ballet dancer. Instead she took the Royal Academy teachers' examinations and started her dancing school. She called it the Deen School of Dancing.

Because Miss Deen had been trained by her aunt, who had been a dancer in Pavlova's company, she believed in strict discipline. When Anna came to her first class she looked her over carefully to see she was properly dressed. She had explained at the interview that all her pupils wore white tunics and, while they were small, socks. 'Later,' she had said, 'if you are still learning with me you will wear a leotard and tights. Leotards are knitted garments rather like a swim suit which all dancers wear for practice. Always take your socks or tights home to wash after each class. These must be made of cotton or wool so they will absorb sweat. The moment your class is over— change. Never sit around in clothes damp from sweat. My classes are bigger than I approve, so be careful never to waste a second. Attend all the time, even when I am talking to another pupil, there is always something you can learn. I believe in good manners, you will call me Madame and at the beginning and end of a class you will make a *révérence* and say before the class "Good afternoon, Madame" and after the class "Thank you, Madame". Now go and line up with the class waiting to come in.'

Above: girl's révérence

That first lesson Anna learnt the first position. The whole class was spaced beside the *barre*. A *barre* in dancing is a hand rail. This is fastened to the wall. It is used by all dancers at practice and for limbering up. The *barre* they were told was to help their balance only, they were never, never to use it to lean on. At home, if they wanted to practise an exercise, they would find their bed rail or perhaps the back of an armchair made a good *barre*. Anything solid, easy to hold on to and at waist-level would do.

For the first position they had to put their heels together and turn out their feet as far as they could. It might be they could not turn their feet right out seeing it was a first lesson, but they were also to learn to turn their legs out as far as their hips. 'Turning out your hips,' Madam explained, 'is called your "turn-out". This is probably something you will hear me talk about at each class. For without good turn-out you will never be a dancer.'

The next exercise Anna learnt at her first lesson was called a *demi-plié*. For the first position they had held on to the *barre* with first the left hand and then the right. For the *demi-plié* they had to face the *barre* and hold on with both hands. Then, with their feet in the first position and their knees turned out, they had to bend their knees slowly, turning outward from their hips while both feet remained flat on the floor. It was hard to do this because it seemed natural to raise the heels. Madam said *pliés* were as much a part of a dancer's life as tights. All dancers, however talented, worked at *pliés* every day.

The class lasted one hour. Part of the time the children worked in the middle of the studio and learnt breathing exercises and simple jumps and some arm exercises. At the end of the class they were taught to make a *révérence*. This was a kind of bow done with the back leg turned out as for a *demi-plié*, while the front leg was stretched forward with the toe pointed; the arms were held out to each side. When they made the *révérence* to Madame before they went home each child, as she bowed, said 'Thank you, Madame'.

Peter was to go to the boys' class. Madame did not like teaching boys and girls together for they needed different qualities. She also liked her boy pupils to start their training under a man. Before his first class Madame told Peter about his teacher.

'He was trained for acrobatics and tumbling, but in his teens he decided to become a dancer. He learnt with very good teachers but always what he was supremely good at was mime, particularly comic mime; he is a master at expressing himself with his whole

Boy's révérence

A pupil at the Bolshoi Ballet School exercising at the barre *to increase her extension by gently stretching muscles and ligaments*

body and of course with his face. When he gave up dancing professionally he settled down near here, and I was indeed fortunate to get him to teach you boys. For from him you will learn dancing and mime. He likes to be called Eduardo. One word from me. You have come to me to learn to dance. You may learn only for a short while and then decide a dancing career is not for you. But make up your mind that whether you learn for a few terms or go all the way to finish up a professional dancer, you will gain qualities of untold value. You will carry yourself better. You will have body control and breath control. You will hold your head straight and high. You will have learnt chivalry. Above all, you will walk tall and with pride.'

Peter was so impressed by all this that he managed a sort of bow as he said 'Thank you, Madame'.

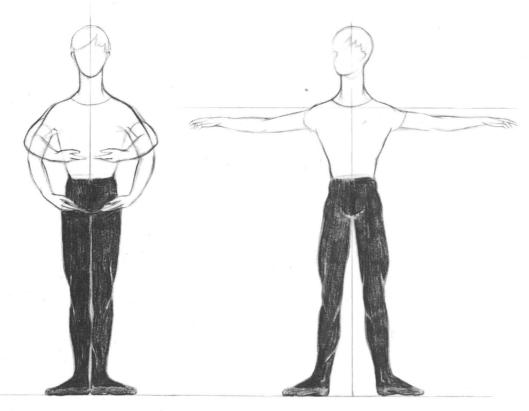

First position   *Second position*

Peter's classes were in some ways like Anna's. He learnt the five positions and he learnt *pliés*. First, as Anna had done, he practised *demi-pliés* and then *grands pliés*. These were just like *demi-pliés*, but you had to continue to go down by lifting the heels when you could go no further in the *demi*. Both *pliés* had to be performed with the knees well out and the bottom tucked well under you.

Eduardo was almost pleased (he was never quite pleased) with Peter's first *grand plié*. 'Work at that, Peter,' he said, 'doing that exercise will do wonders for your ankles.'

Anna and Peter attended ballet classes twice a week after school. But on Saturdays Anna learnt a different kind of dancing. For this class the boys joined the girls, so Peter would have been there too if he had not been playing football. The dancing was called folk dancing.

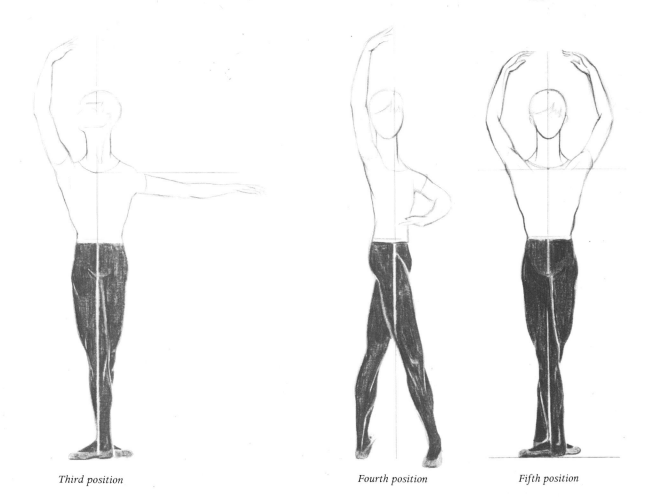

Third position   *Fourth position*   *Fifth position*

'This class,' Madame explained to Anna, 'is partly for co-ordination. What you are learning at the *barre* is disciplined technique. What you learn on Saturdays is relaxed dancing: how to start, how to run, how to move; the steps are simple and natural. What you are going to start learning today is called a running set. When you can dance a running set perfectly you will be nearly a dancer.'

Anna enjoyed folk dancing. It was different and you had to think hard, but when you had learnt the steps it was somehow beautiful because it was simple.

One Saturday, after they had worked at the running set, Miss Deen told the children to sit on the floor.

'I want to talk to you about dancing. What you are learning is the very early training in ballet; but that is a comparatively new way of dancing. People have always danced; dancing is as natural as

19

Left: ancient Greek dancing depicted on a vase in the British Museum which shows the Bacchante celebrating the grape harvest

Below: a sequence of three movements in a popular Egyptian figure-dance in which the partners held hands and, after performing a series of movements, ended by turning each other around

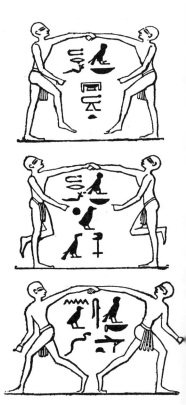

breathing. In museums and books you can see ancient pottery and vases, sculpture and wall paintings showing dancers as they were thousands of years ago. And if you get the opportunity to watch dancers from the Far East, you may see dances performed today just as they have been for thousands of years. These are ritual dances, inspired mainly by religion, so the dancer is trained to use every part of his body to worship or to ask. Asking for things—rain or the end of a plague, for example—was very often a feature of ancient ritual dancing. Still today in ballet you will find we use the same hand movements for pleading.' Madame raised her hands in an asking position. 'Such gestures have been part of most primitive dances.

'We cannot know very much about the music and instruments men used in early civilizations, but because rhythm is a part of all dancing there would always be some form of percussion to mark the beat. The Egyptians had their favourite belongings buried with them when they died, so that they would be to hand in their new life. From these treasures, and from their tomb paintings, we know they had castanets, cymbals, tambourines, drums, pipes and a type of clacker. They also had lyres. I expect they used these together with singers when they danced. From the four little guardian goddesses found in the tomb of Tutankhamun, we may be sure they had exquisite girls from which to choose their dancers.

'Dances can usually be divided into two types: those based on religion and those for entertainment. But there is another type, to crush down bad memories of mass death and destruction and to express the urge for new life. This kind of dancing happened after the Black Death—the plague that swept through Europe during the Middle Ages—and it happens after wars. There was an example of it after the Second World War. A bomb had been dropped on a large store, killing everybody in it. At the time the relatives seemed stunned with grief. Then peace came to Europe. On the night when peace was declared, relations and friends of those who had died in the store, rushed to the spot where the bomb had fallen and danced "Knees Up Mother Brown" and so on all night, shouting and screaming in apparent defiance towards the sky.'

Madame signalled to the children to get up. 'That's as much as I have time for today. I will tell you some more about the beginnings of dancing another Saturday. Now let us tackle the running set.'

Below: ancient Chinese temple-dancing, from a stone-rubbing in the Tun Huan caves

CHAPTER TWO

Positions

Learning to dance was as satisfying as Anna had thought it would be, but, except for Saturday morning class, it was all hard work and no fun. Anna had now learnt all five positions and several exercises, but there it seemed to her she had stuck. Each lesson was exactly like the last one. The children—there were twenty of them—wearing their practice shoes with spotless socks lined up outside the studio door. Then, on a signal that Madame was ready, they marched into their class, each pausing to make a *révérence* to Madame and say 'Good afternoon'. Mostly Madame acknowledged this with a little bow, but sometimes she stopped a child to make some small criticism of her appearance.

'You must get something done about your hair, Sybil. Either plait it and fasten the plaits on top of your head or tie it back in a net. I must be able to see your head and shoulders.'

'Go and look at yourself in the glass, Doris. Your posture is terrible. Look at those humped shoulders, look at your stomach, you must tighten those stomach muscles. Remember, all of you, standing and walking properly is a must for a dancer. Keep those shoulders down and your chin and head up.' At each class, as she made her *révérence*, Anna was scared Madame would criticize something about her that was wrong, but it had not happened yet.

After they had made their *révérence* the children lined up facing the *barre* and the pianist struck a chord. This was the cue for the children to place both hands on the *barre*, put their heels together and turn out their feet for the first position. Then, with their knees well turned out and their tails tucked in, they did four *grands pliés*. While they did the exercise Madame walked up and down behind them studying each child carefully.

'Don't strain to get down further than you comfortably can,' she would say. 'Keeping the knees over the toes, go as deep as possible while being thorough. You will go down deep in time. Always remember, if you become a dancer, this is an exercise you will do every day of your life.'

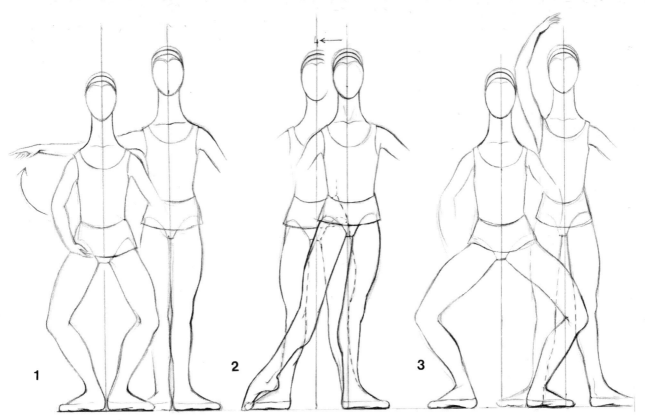

(1) Demi-plié in first position

(2) Extension of the right foot to the second position

(3) Demi-plié in second position

1   **2**   **3**

After the *grands pliés* the pianist played another chord. This was their cue to take their right hand off the *barre* and start on the positions. After the first position came, of course, the second.

This Anna had learnt was like the first only you slid your right foot to the side about one foot length apart from the stationary foot. You were supposed to keep your weight evenly on both feet, which should be in a straight line under your body.

Anna could not yet turn her feet right out, but she knew she had to try to, for Madame had explained that only by being able to turn her feet right out would her turn-out improve. Feet were terribly important in the second position.

'Be careful, Anna, not to let your feet roll inward. Be sure always to feel that your little toe is on the floor.'

Anna felt rather sorry for the third position for it seemed to her everybody snubbed it.

'You must know the third position,' Madame said, 'as it is part of the sequence, but it is mainly used by younger students to help them master the fifth.

'Starting from the second position, you pull your right foot in so it lies beside the left foot. Both feet are supposed to be turned well out.'

1　　　　　　　　　　　　　**2**

Left: (1) grand plié *in second position, (2)* demi-plié *in fifth position*

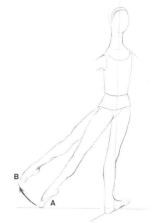

Above and right: three basic extensions—A battement tendu, *B* battement glissé, *C* grand battement derrière

Anna hated the fourth position because it was so difficult to do. You had to slide your right foot forward until the heel of the right foot was in line with the toe of the left foot. Madame was always saying: 'Never, never look at your feet, it throws your position all wrong.' But, Anna worried, how could you know the toe of your left foot was in line with the heel of the right if you didn't look?

Madame would see Anna's face and laugh. 'A dancer,' she said, 'should at all times look serene,' and then she would imitate Anna's anxious, straining expression. 'Look serene, Anna. If you work, the fourth position will come right in the end.'

The fifth position, which many of the class found difficult, Anna did not mind. You had to slide your right foot so it lay flat beside the left foot. Of course the toes should have been perfectly turned out, which Anna could not yet manage, but she did keep her knees

Above: stretching the Achilles' tendon

perfectly straight. This was what was difficult for many of the others because their front knees would try and bend.

After the positions came more *pliés*, this time with the feet in each of the positions. These were very hard work for there was so much to remember. The second position was the only one where the heels must not leave the floor. In the fourth position the back knee was the trouble, it would point inward and towards the ground. In the fifth the heels were the trouble. You had to feel them pushing to come up while you were trying to push them down. Madame was always talking about heels and ankles. 'This exercise', she would say, 'will strengthen your Achilles' tendon which is of vital importance to a dancer.'

They also learnt something called *battement tendu*. This was a little sliding extension, first with one leg and then with the other. The tip of the toe had to be well pointed and remain on the floor. Both knees had to be absolutely straight. The girls were supposed to feel that the arches of the foot were lifted up—Anna was not sure she felt this—and the heels had to be well turned out. Like all the other exercises it meant a lot of thinking. When they had learnt *battements tendus* to the side they performed them to the front and to the back.

Then there was the *battement jeté*, again to the front, sides and back. It was like the *battement tendu*, only for this exercise the extended foot with the pointed toe rose about two inches from the floor.

On the day when the class danced the running set well enough for Madame to say 'Not bad' she again told the children to sit on the floor.

'Last time I was talking about dancing history, I told you just a little about primitive dancing. A lot has been written on this subject. I can recommend *The Dance* by Agnes de Mille, who is a dancer turned choreographer. This means that as well as knowing all the dancer's problems she knows the problems of actually planning the movements of dances, which is what the choreographer does. The problems of the dancer are very different from the problems of the choreographer, but it is worth while to understand both.

'All over Mediaeval Europe the peasants had some form of folk dancing. Of course the sort of dancing they did varied enormously from country to country. In England almost all the dancing was for everybody to join in, with no leaders. It was simple, with running steps like you are learning, or jigging steps, but nothing like the slapping and stamping that you will see if ever you watch the folk

Engraving by Albrecht Dürer of Mediaeval peasants dancing

The Gopak, a Ukranian dance in the acrobatic style typical of Eastern European folk dancing

dancing of Germanic countries, or the squatting acrobatic solos of countries in Eastern Europe. I have purposely spoken of ''English'' folk dancing, for presumably the Scots were dancing early forms of their reels to their bagpipes, which are very old instruments indeed, used in ancient times by both Hebrews and Greeks. The hardy Highlanders were skirled into battle by the bagpipes and when victorious, usually against the English, they would celebrate their success by dancing reels. Not probably as danced today, when the foot-work is immensely elegant, but wild savage dances to express joy.

'As well as folk dancing, in which men, women and children danced together, Mediaeval England also had its Morris dancers. These were all men, and they not only danced but performed a sort of play. The characters were roughly the same all over the country: there was a hobby horse, often a dragon, a man-woman figure and, in some places, a barber or a surgeon. In many parts of England you can still see Morris dancing. Nowadays it is just rough fun, but in its beginnings it was not fun at all. Those elaborate sword dances performed by today's Morris men, in their early days finished with somebody's head being cut off and carried round in triumph on the crossed swords.

27

'Dancing is and always was taken very seriously in Spain. Spaniards often dance alone or in pairs. Their dancing, with its beauty, its heavily marked rhythm and its excitement appealed to another race of dancers—the gypsies, a wild, passionate people who brought Eastern and Western dancing together. In Spain the gypsies created a style of dancing called the Flamenco. A festival of Flamenco dancing is held every year in Spain.

'Dancing in court circles in Mediaeval Europe was based on the local folk dancing of the ordinary people, but was formalized, with all the roughness and horse-play cut out. In fact dancing in court circles was much more formal and exact than it has ever been since. There was no improvisation on dance floors as there is today. Mediaeval court dancing had two main purposes: first, showing off and, secondly, courtship.

'Nobody was ever grander than the gallants of the day. They were brought up to believe they were the salt of the earth, owing allegiance to none but their emperor or king. These men, so sure of their beauty, really did look splendid even just standing around, and the ladies dressed with real elegance to match. Their heavy velvet skirts touching the floor cannot have made dancing easy, but dance they did, even if they left the freer movements to their partners.

'Court dancing, as you will see, was the very, very beginning of dancing as we know it today. As the years passed, dancing became part of the training of courtiers. On another Saturday morning I will tell you a little about dancing at royal courts.'

Right: La Délivrance de Renaud, a spectacular court 'ballet' in which Louis XIII took part when it was first performed in the Louvre, Paris, in 1617

Left: the Galliard, a lively dance popular in the late-sixteenth and early-seventeenth century—the woodcut is from Thoinot Arbeau's Orchésographie, a French handbook on dances of the period, published in 1588

17

CHAPTER THREE

Anna Meets Peter

Anna was now moving on again. She still had to do *pliés* in all the positions, breathing exercises, simple arm movements, and *battements*, but now for the first time she was learning to do an exercise in the middle of the room. Madame called this 'centre work'.

'You won't be able to do this well yet,' she said, 'but I do want you to learn to balance without the *barre* to hold on to. Some of you grip it as if you were going down on a sinking ship. Now this is a *pirouette*.'

Madame raised herself on one foot *demi-pointe*, then she put the other foot in a well turned out position on the ankle of the foot on which she was standing. Then, light as a feather, she spun round in a sequence of turns.

The class was enchanted; this was real dancing, such a glorious change from hanging on to that old *barre*.

'Now,' said Madame, 'raise that left foot *demi-pointe* and don't let the other dangle; turn it well out and place it across the knee of the raised foot. Now don't hurry but let me see one spin.'

It was too tempting. All the girls longed to *pirouette* like Madame. So they did not stop at one spin but tried to do several. But of course

Right: Merle Park dances a pirouette in Romeo and Juliet

Left: the different stages of a pirouette

they were not ready for it; they all staggered and three, including Anna, fell over. Madame laughed.

'I said one *pirouette*. Now try again.'

It could not be said the *pirouettes* were well done but, as Madame said, the great thing was to feel they knew how to do them. 'In future you will do a little centre practice for the feet as well as for the arms at each class. Now, after that excitement, let me see and hear you breathe.'

The breathing exercises they had to do at every class. They stood in the middle of the studio in two rows. Then, as Madame counted

Ballet performance organized by Catherine de Medici in 1573 in honour of the Polish ambassador. Detail from a contemporary woodcut

up to four, with their lips closed they took a huge breath. This they had to hold by control from their diaphragms while Madame again counted up to four. Finally, slowly to another count of four, they opened their mouths and let the big breath go.

That next Saturday Madame told the class some more about the history of dancing. The children sat on the floor, while she herself sat very upright in a chair. Nobody that the children knew had a back as straight as Madame's.

'Last time I talked to you about ballet history, I was telling you about the elegant dancing that became fashionable in court circles throughout Mediaeval Europe. But from 1400 onwards the real centre of "ballet" performances was Italy—though the wildly extravagant performances of that time were not what we should call "ballets". They were more like pageants, a mixture of everything: acting, music, poetry and dancing, and everybody who was anybody in court circles took part.

'Then in 1519 a baby was born to a rich influential Italian family. Her name was Catherine de Medici. As she grew up, as a matter of course, she took part in the ballet pageants and enjoyed them enormously. So when she married Henry II of France and found there were no ballet pageants at the French Court, she decided to organize some.

'Catherine's first ballet pageant was about Circe, an enchantress who turned men into animals. It lasted five hours and had an audience of ten thousand enormously influential people from all over Europe to watch it. Of course the influential wrote home describing what they had seen and this encouraged others to put on huge showy performances of their own. Soon learning to dance was accepted as an important part of the education of the aristocracy and the wealthy. Even kings took part in the dancing entertainments.

'It was when Louis XIV came to the throne of France that dancing rose to a new height. For he not only danced himself, but sponsored the first ballet school in Europe. This was attached, in 1672, to the Académie Royale de Musique—the Royal Academy of Music—which had been founded three years earlier. The school was open to students from all walks of life, and it was here that the first women dancers were trained. Previously all the female rôles in the ballet pageants had been danced by men, while the court ladies were used simply as decorative background. It is because the first ballet school was in France that all the ballet steps which you are learning have French names.

'Louis XIV did not just learn to dance when he was a child, he went on learning for twenty years. His dancing master was called Beauchamps and Louis had a lesson with him every day.' Madame smiled as she saw in her mind's eye Beauchamps with his royal pupil. 'You are, I expect, wondering what the King learnt during twenty years of lessons. Nobody knows exactly, but from pictures painted at the time we can get a good idea. You remember I told you a little about Scotland's reels. Now, if you get a chance, watch a Scots regiment marching. It is so beautiful it can bring tears to your eyes, for their bodies are perfectly positioned. The legs are absolutely straight, the arms and the head work together. In fact, though if you boys told them so I think they might give you a beating, they all have the beautiful positioning of ballet dancers. And this is just what Beauchamps tried to achieve when he was teaching Louis XIV, for this perfect positioning made him move at all times like a king.

'Once Louis had mastered the perfect position, Beauchamps taught him steps, very elegant, with the toe exquisitely pointed. He taught him to jump; this is called *élévation* and is glorious to watch and to perform. But at that time the clothes of the wealthy were made of exquisite materials and, when there was a court performance, they were coated with jewels and had superb trains added. As a result the men moved with more dignity than agility, while the women could scarcely move at all. So Louis turned to his ballet school. Why not engage the dancers from there to do anything particularly fancy, while leaving beauty and elegance to himself and his Court. The idea was good, and of course the pupils were delighted, but Louis did not know something we all know today. The gap between amateurs and professionals is enormous; the two never join forces and always in the end the professionals take over. This is what happened in France. Next time I shall tell you about some of the professional dancers.'

It was that Saturday that Anna and Peter met.

Lunch had to be late on Saturdays to give Anna time to get home from the dancing school. As she sat down at the table her mother said, 'I'm going to tea with Mrs Brown this afternoon. She has a nephew and niece staying for the night. She asked me to bring you and she's invited a boy, so there'll be four of you.'

Anna had known her mother was going out to tea, so she had planned to practise her positions in her parents' bedroom where the only long glass in the house lived. She was not really allowed to work in her parents' room, so she jumped at chances when they turned up.

Galina Ulanova and Nicolai Fadeyechev rehearsing élévation

'Oh no! Must I go? I have homework.' This wasn't exactly a lie, for after all dancing practice was sort of homework.

But her mother was firm. 'Nonsense! You never have much homework and you can do it tomorrow. I promised Mrs Brown I'd bring you and Daddy has promised to look after the little ones.'

That afternoon the four children met. The Brown children rather shy and Peter and Anna looking cross because they did not want to be there. It was a nice day so the children were given a picnic tea in the garden and over the food they all relaxed. The conversation as usual turned to schools.

'Do you like yours?' the Brown girl whose name was Amanda asked Anna. Anna thought about that.

'Sort of, but I go as well to a dancing school and I wish it was a place where I could do ordinary lessons too.'

Peter stared at Anna. 'Do you? So do I. I go to the Deen School of Dancing.'

'Goodness!' said the Brown boy whose name was Robin. 'I didn't know boys went to dancing schools.'

Peter gave him a dirty look.

'They do. But at my other school I learn boxing, and I can hit.'

'I go to the Deen School too,' Anna said. 'Why don't you come on Saturdays? Lots of your class do.'

'Because I play football,' Peter explained. 'They think I may be in the team. But there's no football next term so I shall go then.'

Anna left out about the folk dancing in case Robin sounded rude again.

'Often Madame tells us ballet history. It's awfully interesting.'

Amanda would have liked to hear more about the dancing school, but she could see her brother was just waiting to get at Peter. So she said, 'If nobody wants any more tea, let's play hide and seek. I vote you go and hide, Robin.'

Looking for Robin, Anna and Peter got together.

'I'll tell my mother about you,' Anna whispered. 'Perhaps you could come to tea and then you could show me what you learn and I'll show you what we do. At least I'll try to but I'm not any good yet.'

'Nor me,' said Peter, 'but I'd like to come to tea. I've nobody at home who's really interested in dancing.'

CHAPTER FOUR

Music

Peter's father was a doctor and his mother was tied to the house by three small children, one a baby. Although neither was interested in ballet, they were both musical—his father played the fiddle and his mother had a good soprano voice; they got great pleasure from their own talents and knew how relaxing music could be.

'I suppose,' Peter's father had said, when they had first decided to let Peter go to the Deen School, 'he hopes to get the same kick out of dancing as I get from my quartet nights or you get singing in the church choir. It may be only a passing phase but let's give him his head.'

Anna's father was a vet who had started out as a caddy, so his great hobby was playing golf. She too had younger brothers and sisters, so her mother was also tied to the house. She could not imagine why Anna wanted to dance. Many a time she wished she had not sent Anna to stay with the godmother who took her to see her first ballet, but now and again she felt a twinge of shame. It was really hard on Anna when she came home bursting to tell somebody what Madame had said, or to explain a new exercise that she had learnt, that all she got was a 'Yes, dear' or 'Very nice, dear', which a child far less intelligent than Anna would interpret as 'Mother is not even listening'. So, when on their way home from the Browns Anna told her about Peter also going to the ballet school, she was pleased, though with reservations, for really it was very odd a boy learning dancing. Still, he looked a nice boy. Perhaps he was learning to dance for health reasons. Anyway it would be good for Anna to have a dancer friend to talk to.

'You had better telephone him when we get in. Perhaps he could come to tea tomorrow.'

From then onwards either Saturday or Sunday afternoons, sometimes both, the children spent together and compared notes. Both Madame and Eduardo were against much practice at improvised *barres* where faults might be acquired, but both approved of mime and dancing to get the feel of music and find out what it had to say. Now and again Peter and Anna taught each other new things they had learnt. Anna, at her centre practice, was learning to jump lightly but not too high and the *pas de bourrée*, which was a sort of little run. Peter, on the other hand, was learning to jump as high as he could, changing his feet in the air. This was called *changement de pieds*. Anna was envious of Peter, for his jumps with foot changes looked much grander than anything she was learning, so for fun she practised Peter's jumps. Soon she was changing feet just as well as Peter did. Neither of them was very good but they felt they were, which they thought was what mattered.

But what they did a great deal when they were together was mime as Peter was being taught by Eduardo.

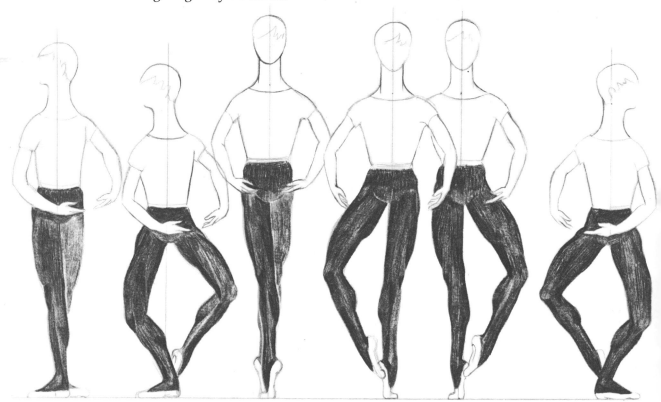

'We have to do it all over,' Peter explained, 'with our faces and with our whole bodies, but what we've mostly learnt so far is what we do with our hands.' Then he clasped his fingers together. 'This is imploring for something.' Then he stretched one hand full out.

The different stages of a pas de bourrée

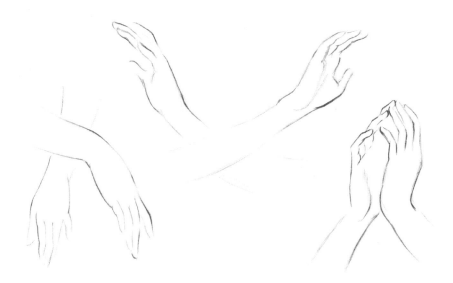

Hand gestures 'This is disgust or loathing. Eduardo says there is a whole language of things you say with your hands, but most of them are the natural gestures exaggerated that people use in real life. When Eduardo worked with a circus and was a clown he was always the one to have water tipped over him or be pushed around, so his hands—and of course the rest of him too—were always saying "Please don't". He showed us and he was so good he made us feel sorry for him.'

One Saturday afternoon Peter told Anna that they had learnt some mime which told a story.

'Have you heard of a play by Shakespeare called *A Midsummer Night's Dream*?'

Anna nodded. 'When I first went to school the older girls acted it. I was a fairy.'

'Well, it's been made into a ballet. Do you know the story?'

'Not really, only about the King and Queen of the Fairies quarrelling about a little Indian boy.'

'I didn't know about that,' Peter admitted, 'but Eduardo told us about what he called the comics. They want to act a play for the Duke's wedding. But when they are rehearsing in a wood one of them, who is called Bottom, has an ass's head put on him by a sort of fairy called Puck. Then Titania, the Queen of the Fairies, who has been asleep, wakes up and falls in love with Bottom.'

'It sounds a silly sort of ballet to me,' said Anna.

'It does rather,' Peter agreed, 'but it's what happens at the end that's interesting. For it all turns out to be a sort of dream and Bottom tries to remember what happened. Eduardo says in the

39

dream bit, when Bottom was wearing his ass's head, the man who danced the part danced on his *pointes* like a girl.'

'Goodness!' said Anna. 'I didn't know men could.'

'Well this one did, but what Eduardo thought was super was after the dream part was over and Bottom tried to remember what had happened. Eduardo said in the play Bottom was helped by words, but of course in the ballet it was all mime.' Peter tried to show Anna what Eduardo had shown the class. 'First he felt for his long ass's ears. Then for the fur which had been all over his face. Then he saw his great clumsy feet and was confounded. Was it possible those same great feet had once danced delicate steps? No, it was past believing.'

After showing the class Bottom's miming, Eduardo had said, 'That was lovely miming, that was.' Then he had smacked his lips as if after a good meal.

The children did most of their miming when they were in Anna's house, for she had no music to which they could practise dancing. Peter's father had a tape recorder which he had lent Peter to take to one of his classes. Peter, who had been given a cassette for Christmas, had put his father's recorder on the floor of the studio and shoved in the microphone and had managed to get a good recording of one whole class—both the music and what Eduardo said. His father wouldn't often let Peter take his recorder out of the house, but he allowed him to plug in his own cassette when Anna came to tea.

There was a different pianist for Peter's classes than there was for Anna's. Anna, listening to the music of Peter's class, remarked on this.

'Yours is the worst one,' Peter said. 'Eduardo calls her Miss Thumpty Thump. The one who plays for us plays for all Madame's morning classes. She can't come every afternoon.'

'It's not fair really,' Anna said, as she watched Peter doing *demi-pliés* to Chopin's *Les Sylphides* music. 'I could do my *pliés* better with nice music.'

'The bit I like Dad says comes from *Peter and the Wolf*. But Eduardo says the best ballet for mime is *Petrouchka*. I'm saving up to buy another cassette to record that when we learn it.'

'You've got a piano,' Anna pointed out. 'Why don't you learn to play that?'

'I am,' Peter said. 'Mum's teaching me, but when I'm playing my feet want to dance.'

Alexander Grant on pointes *as Bottom in Frederick Ashton's ballet* The Dream, *which is based on Shakespeare's* A Midsummer Night's Dream

40

Anna sighed. 'I think you're lucky. All I have is a recorder to play on and that's kept at school.'

'Couldn't you ask Madame what you could do to hear music for dancing?' Peter suggested.

Anna gasped. 'Goodness no. I'd never dare. I'll just have to think about the music I hear in your house.'

As it happened, at her very next dancing class Madame spoke to Anna. She stopped her after her class *révérence*.

'Go and change, Anna, then come back here. I want to speak to you.'

Anna, though she whispered 'Yes, Madame', felt as if ice were slipping down her back. It was well known that Madame advised children to leave her school if she thought they were wasting their time. She had now been learning for nearly a term, which was probably long enough for Madame to see if she showed any promise. She was made even more despondent by those girls who had overheard what Madame had said. They looked at her as if Madame had said she had the plague.

But when ten minutes later, dressed for home, Anna came back into the studio, Madame did not look at all fierce; in fact she smiled when Anna, encumbered by wellingtons, her school overcoat, an umbrella, and a plastic bag containing some of her dancing clothes which needed washing and a towel, soap and talcum powder, struggled to make a *révérence*. 'Don't try to do that now,' she said. 'What I want to talk about is your hair.'

Anna was a pale child with large grey eyes which very easily looked worried. Her great beauty was her hair which was a deep chestnut colour, curled slightly, and fell nearly to her waist. All the girls had to fasten their hair back so that Madame could see their necks and shoulders. Because Anna had so much hair, she plaited it in a thick rope, tying it with a neat bow. She had always known that there might be trouble about her hair—even plaited it seemed to get in the way. She looked at Madame her eyes full of worry. How could she make Madame understand she could not cut her hair off without sounding conceited? She knew that what Madame wanted was more important than what they wanted at home, but Dad and Mum didn't. They were proud of her hair.

'I want to have it cut off but Mum won't let me.'

Anna wore her hair loose to go home; Madame picked up a strand of it and let it slide through her fingers. 'Cut off!' she said, sounding shocked. 'I should hope not indeed. But I must be able to see your

Port de bras—the girls have their hair pinned up in a 'coronet'

neck and shoulders. I was wondering if you could manage to wear it in two plaits pinned to your head in a sort of coronet. It may not be possible, it may be too heavy and fall down. Then we might consider a net. But never, never think of cutting it off. If you decide on a career in dancing you will need long hair later on.'

Anna thought her interview was over and was turning to go but Madame stopped her. 'Are you happy learning dancing?'

'Oh yes, Madame.'

'I think sometimes you find the *barre* exercises a bore.'

Anna was shocked into speaking her mind. 'Oh no, Madame. Not the exercises. Just I don't awfully like the music. There's a boy called Peter who goes to the boy's class and he's made a recording of their music and it's much nicer than ours.'

Madame looked pleased. 'You're quite right. I don't like "Tiptoe through the Tulips" either, but good pianists are hard to come by. With luck, you may get the same pianist as Peter next term.'

Galina Ulanova in Les Sylphides

CHAPTER FIVE

Watching Ballet

A good ballet company was going to visit the town. Madame told the whole school well in advance about it. She had, she told them, made a provisional booking. She also told them what the seats would cost.

'It sounds rather a lot but the seats are in the front row of the dress circle. Always try and watch ballet from the circles, never if you can help it watch from the stalls. Ballet is not meant to be watched from below.'

That term Anna's class was given the same good pianist as Peter's class had. Anna was very glad they had her, for now quite a lot of their time was spent on what the class called arm exercises and Madame called *port de bras*. This was part of centre practice. For the exercise the pianist played a tune Anna loved. She did not know, but it was a practice version of a dance from *Les Sylphides*.

For the *port de bras* you put your feet in any classical position. Anna could turn her feet out properly now, without them rolling and with her little toe on the floor, so she could manage a good fifth position.

To start *port de bras* the right foot was in front and the right shoulder a shade in front of the left. The arms hung down but the wrists were curled inward so that the finger tips touched. From this position, counting four in time to the music, you slowly raised your arms as high as your waist.

What was difficult about this was that the elbows should scarcely bend at all. Instead the arms should curve softly, the hands facing each other and the fingers nearly touching. At every class Madame would call out, 'Think of your elbows, girls. Oh Anna, those elbows! Oh Susan, do try to remember those elbows!'

From that position, again counting in time to the music, the class lifted their arms shoulder high, then spread them wide open, the palms of the hands facing the front wall. The arms were then raised to above the head, a little forward of the face. Then, still counting a-one and a-two and a-three and a-four, the arms were lowered to the starting position.

'*Les Sylphides* is perhaps the most important ballet for the *port de bras*,' Madame said. 'I expect you often think you waste a lot of time on your arms when you would rather be dancing with your feet. If you see *Sylphides* you will know why. The girls who dance in the *corps de ballet*—the ordinary members of the company who do not dance solos— in this ballet have to use their arms as if they were leaves stirred by a breeze: not a bone in them.'

Madame and Eduardo gave their pupils rules to remember. These were to be said out loud three or four times a day. Each was in the form of a question: 'Am I standing equally on both my feet?' 'Are my muscles holding in my tummy while I control my breath?' 'Are my shoulders down?' 'Is my head straight and high?'

I can't say Peter and Anna always stood and walked perfectly positioned, but at least they tried, and certainly their posture had improved since they had started to learn to dance.

One day Madame got a poster about the visiting ballet company. She pinned it up on the board in the entrance hall. It told them they would see two ballets on the Saturday afternoon. They were *Le Spectre de la Rose*, then an interval, then *La Fille Mal Gardée*.

On the next Saturday morning after folk dancing Madame told the class to sit down and she would tell them something about the ballets they were to see.

Madame sat in her usual straight-backed position, but her eyes looked as though she was seeing what she described.

'*Le Spectre de la Rose*, which means the vision of a rose, is danced

Leslie Edwards and Alexander Grant in Frederick Ashton's version of La Fille Mal Gardée— *the photograph shows the importance of mime and make-up, used here to portray an affluent farmer and his simple-minded son who is a suitor to Lise*

to music you may have heard, for it is very well known as Weber's "Invitation to the Waltz" '. The original scenery and the clothes were designed by a great theatrical designer called Léon Bakst. The dance was planned—choreographed—by Michel Fokine. It was in the days of the great Diaghilev company, which I shall be telling you about when we get on to dancing in the twentieth century. It was designed for two of his leading dancers—Madame Karsavina and Vaslav Nijinsky, who were an enormous success. The ballet is seldom danced now. I think it is felt it was so beautiful as it was danced in Diaghilev's day that it should not be attempted by anybody else.

'The man's part in *Spectre de la Rose* is the spirit of a rose which is given to a young girl at a ball. In her sleep the girl dances with her rose. It should be a lovely ballet for you to watch, for it is full of beautiful movements for both the girl and the boy.

'*La Fille Mal Gardée*, which means the girl who was not well enough guarded, is entirely different. It is a very old ballet and is delightful to watch as well as being very funny. It is a village romp about Lise a farmer's daughter and her boy friend Colin. Lise's mother has other ideas about who her daughter shall marry. There is a lot of charming dancing, including a very amusing clog dance, and I know you will enjoy it.'

Somehow, in many cases by doing without something else, all the children learning at the Deen School managed to raise the money for their theatre seats. Peter's father made Peter pay for his own ticket out of his pocket money.

'It's up to you if you want to go to the ballet,' his father explained, 'but I'm not made of money and you're not an only child. I'd be ruined if all my children wanted theatre seats.'

Anna's father paid for her seat, but he took the money off her next birthday present.

'You'll be ten in September and I had hoped to buy you the tape recorder you want. But that will probably have to wait until Christmas if you need that theatre seat.'

Anna discussed this with Peter. 'Most of the girls in my class seem to have simply masses of pocket money. I only get 10p and that has to buy things for dancing like talcum powder.'

'I get 20p,' said Peter, 'but that has to cover absolutely everything you can think of, including school charities, and they are fierce. I think Dad would make me buy my own practice shoes if I possibly could.'

48

Tamara Karsavina and Vaslav Nijinsky in Le Spectre de la Rose

Anna sighed. 'We are being made to know the value of money. I heard Dad say that to Mum. Dad was educated on scholarships so he knows all about not having money.'

There are many ways of watching ballet. You may, before you go, plan to watch for steps you have learnt in class. You may just let the beauty slide over you as though you are floating in a warm sea. Madame made no suggestions. She left it to each child to get all they could out of the matinée.

'I make only two rules,' she said. 'The first is nobody is to say one word while the ballet is in progress. And the other is no one is to eat while the curtain is up. You will notice the ill-educated bringing packets and even boxes of chocolates and sweets to the theatre, and unwrapping them during the performance, so that the crackle of paper disturbs everyone. I do not mind a sweet eaten, or even an ice, in the interval, but only in the interval.'

The ballet company was good even by Madame's standards. If perhaps Madame occasionally remembered wistfully other greater performances she had seen, she also reminded herself this was a young company and what sometimes they lacked in technique they made up for in verve and dash.

The whole school was dumbfounded by the glory of what they saw. The rose in *Le Spectre de la Rose* seemed to leap into the girl's bedroom almost to the roof and yet come down as softly as a rose petal. To all the small girls the dancer who danced the girl in the ballet was themselves. As the dancer came into her bedroom in her ball gown and kissed the rose she had been given, then sighed sleepily and fell into her armchair, each girl thought 'That's me'.

NIJINSKY

A contemporary artist's impression of Nijinsky in Le Spectre de la Rose

CHAPTER SIX

The Great Move

Two Saturdays later after a session of folk dancing Madame went
back to the subject of ballet history.

'A dancer who was trained at the Louis XIV ballet school has now
become part of ballet history. Her name was Marie Camargo though
she is generally known as La Camargo. After she left the Royal
Academy she was engaged as a member of the *corps de ballet* at the
Paris Opera. The *corps de ballet*, as you know, is one of the large
groups of dancers who make up a ballet company. That is to say she
never danced solos or even in a group of three or four dancers. What
happened to her is what all members of a ballet company pray will
happen to them. The leading male dancer missed his entrance so the
stage was bare. This was Camargo's chance; she ran on to the stage
and invented a charming little dance to the music of the missing
male dancer.

'At that date—the beginning of the eighteenth century—ballets
were not a bit like they are today. The story was told in many acted
scenes with dancing in between. It was one of these spots Camargo
filled, and it is to be presumed she brought down the house, for from
that moment she was famous. Being famous she was able to do more
or less as she liked and what she did was to have her skirts cut
shorter. Remember I told you women of that time wore their clothes
to the ground. La Camargo had her beautiful dresses raised clear of
the ground so that the audience could see her feet and ankles; as
well, she wore shoes without heels, so that she could jump. She was
a sensation.

'Dancing at this period reminds me of the Olympic torch. As you
may have heard, or seen on television, before each Olympic Games
a torch is carried from one runner to another to light the new Olympic
flame. This was in a way what was happening in the seventeenth,
eighteenth and early nineteenth century in the ballet world. Something new in the technique of dancing was handed on like a torch
from dancer to dancer. The difficulty for me is to pick out who
amongst the many have had the greatest influence.

*An eighteenth-century engraving
of Marie Camargo*

*A cartoon of Auguste Vestris,
made while he was in London*

'During the hundred years between 1730 and 1830 the shape of ballets changed very slowly, or at least it seems that way to us. Yet, of course, the boys and girls who were dancing at that time didn't see things that way. When training there were still exercises to be mastered. They too had goals to reach for. A great male dancer called Vestris was dancing at the end of the eighteenth century. He was apparently a very fine dancer indeed, but he became a torch bearer because of somebody else—Georges Noverre. Always it is interesting when a dancer becomes a choreographer, and that is what Noverre did, using Vestris as his leading dancer. At that time it was customary for the male dancers to wear masks. These, of course, could only show one expression—love or anger for example. Noverre wanted dancing to be more than stylized steps, he wanted the whole body and the face to act. So, starting with Vestris, he did

Detail from a lithograph idealizing Marie Taglioni's lightness of foot by showing her balanced gracefully on a rose—the rose was in fact made of metal

away with masks. He himself had taken acting lessons from David Garrick, the great English actor of that date. Using what he had learnt from David Garrick he produced something quite new—dancing dramas which told a story.

'Now here is another torch bearer. In 1804 a baby girl was born in Stockholm. Her father was the *maître de ballet* and her mother the daughter of a singer, so of course it was expected the little girl would have a future in the theatre. Her name was Marie Taglioni. She started to learn dancing from her father; then, when she was eight years old, she went to learn in Paris. She first danced professionally when she was eighteen.

'Marie Taglioni became a beautiful dancer, famous wherever she danced because of her grace and—something quite new—her lovely line. But, apart from being the most exquisite dancer of her day,

Following page: a painting by Edgar Degas of dancers in a ballet studio of the Opéra in Paris

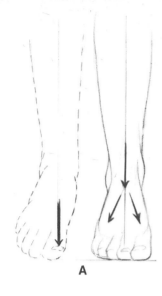

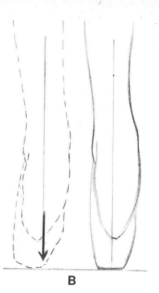

Diagram A shows two feet on demi-pointes; *diagram B shows two feet on full* pointes. *In both A and B the left-hand example illustrates bad distribution of weight with all the pressure resting on the big toe; the right-hand example illustrates good distribution of weight so that the pressure is spread evenly down the centre of the foot and toes*

A

B

Taglioni did something practical towards handing on the dancing torch. You remember I told you Marie Camargo wore flat shoes so that she could jump on the stage. But shoes without heels did not catch on as much as you would expect. All the girls learnt to stand on the tips of their toes, which are called *pointes*, but they could not do much when they got there because their shoes were too soft and hurt their toes. Marie Taglioni thought up something new. She darned the toes of her dancing slippers and strapped her toes for extra support. This made dancing on the *pointes* not only possible, but beautiful to watch. In about two years' time those of you girls who are still learning with me will start to dance on your *pointes*; then out will come your needles and thread and you will find yourself darning your toes just as Marie Taglioni did in the nineteenth century.

'All this time ballet had been centred where it started, in Paris, but now great dancers travelled. Marie Taglioni was a riot in Russia and all over Europe. Though Paris still remained the centre of the dancing world other countries had ballets. In 1840 a dancer called Fanny Elssler danced in America and was such a success that when she was dancing in Washington, Congress was given an afternoon off so that all the senators and congressmen could go to her matinée.

'Dancers were now beginning to move around. An Italian dancer called Carlotta Grisi joined the Paris Opera ballet and was very popular with the Parisians. It was for Grisi that a fine choreographer called Jean Coralli, with help from Jules Perrot who was a dancer, invented the ballet *Giselle*. This is now of course a period piece but it is still most ballerinas' ambition to dance the title rôle.

Fanny Elssler dancing the Cachucha from Le Diable boiteux, *a contemporary print*

'England too was enjoying ballet and no one more than Queen Victoria. She decided in 1845 that she would like to see the greatest ballerinas on the stage at the same time. I have often wondered about this. Queen Victoria is not renowned for her sense of humour, but then it is not a quality a biographer—a person who writes about famous people's lives—looks for in a queen. But I can't help wondering if, through her ladies, Queen Victoria had heard backstage gossip about the jealousy and excitability of star dancers. Anyway she commanded the four starriest to dance a *pas de quatre*, which means a dance for four, for her in London. Thanks to an extraordinarily tactful choreographer, Carlotta Grisi and Fanny Cenito from Italy, Marie Taglioni from Sweden and Denmark's great star Lucille Grahn all appeared together successfully and, as far as is known, without any rows. In fact everybody was pleased. This little story shows how international ballet was becoming.

'Russia did not come to the front of the ballet scene until a dancer from France called Marius Petipa went there in 1847. He really only intended a short visit but instead he became a choreographer and stayed there for the rest of his life. In his lifetime he saw the centre of dancing leave Paris and move to what we now know as Leningrad, but which was then called St Petersburg.' Madame got up. 'There we shall leave ballet history for this term.'

It was nearly the summer holidays when the Deen School would close for five weeks. Next term would be important for both Peter and Anna for they had birthdays, Anna in September and Peter in October. Both would be ten. It made them feel almost grown up to be going into double figures. Madame talked to her whole school about dancing practice during the holiday.

'I don't want any *barre* practice. Five weeks is too long for you to do it alone. You could very easily start a fault without knowing it and this fault might go on getting worse so it would be difficult, perhaps impossible, to cure when your classes start again. Instead what I want you to do is dance. Just turn on your transistors and dance. Don't worry about real steps, just feel what the music is saying to you and dance to it. You will be all over the place, some abroad some at home, but wherever you are, dance.'

Carlotta Grisi and Marius Petipa dance the Waltz in Giselle

CHAPTER SEVEN

Summer Holiday

The summer holiday, as is the habit of summer holidays, passed in a flash. Anna went with her family to stay in a caravan in Devonshire. It was a popular, crowded spot where there was so much to do every day it was difficult to find time to dance in the way Madame had told her to. But she did have one weekend which was nothing but dancing. It was a Folk Festival and for very little money Anna's father bought her a ticket for every session.

Before the festival started Anna had wished so much that Peter were there. She had only learnt a little folk dancing; would she be good enough to join in? If she tried to join in, who would be her partner?

The first session was on the Friday evening; everybody met in a large hall which was quite near the caravan site. The moment she got into the hall Anna could feel she had no need to worry. About three hundred people of all ages, many quite old, were all there for one purpose—to enjoy themselves.

Anna had supposed there would be a band to dance to, or perhaps they would use canned music. There was a band but it was not like any band she had heard before, for there were only a few players. There was a drum which Anna thought was the most important, for it was the rhythmic beat on the drum which set everybody's feet tapping. Then there were fiddles and what gay music they made! There were two accordions and a triangle, and some other instruments Anna had not seen before. On the platform as well as the band, there was a man some people called Joey and others Mr Smith. Anna was told he was the Master of Ceremonies who would call out the names of the dances. Actually, with so many chattering people in the hall, Anna never did hear the name of a dance but, almost as soon as a dance was announced, the band would strike up a gay tune which set every foot in the hall jigging. A man who was partnering people caught hold of Anna's hand and led her to a young man from India who also had no partner, and at once they were dancing with everybody else. It was a dance which had probably been danced in the eighteenth century and was specially designed to fit all ages and all classes, just as it was doing that night. Groups of people all over the hall formed up in lines, then the top two paired off and danced together down to the other end while all the other dancers twirled each other around. Neither Anna nor her partner, whose name sounded like Jamashid, knew that their feet were jigging, just as centuries of other feet had jigged for the sheer love of dancing, but that was what was happening.

Anna and Jamashid danced together for the rest of the evening. Not that they could dance all the dances, some were much too difficult. There was what Anna thought was a reel, which people said came from Dorset; it had such elaborate and beautiful foot-work it might have been danced by professionals.

The evening was not all dancing. There was a sort of play with dancing in the middle. The performers were all men dressed in white with flowers in their hats. Round their knees were fastened strings of bells. They carried handkerchiefs. Both Anna and Jamashid thought the dancing was very good indeed. This was not accompanied by the band, but by one violin.

The play was funny but very difficult to understand because all the actors had strong country accents. The character Anna liked best was a hobby horse.

After this there was a sort of community singing, only instead of popular songs they sang folk songs. Anna and Jamashid did not know the songs, but they enjoyed listening.

Then they were back on the floor dancing to such a lovely rhythm that Anna felt she could have danced for ever.

When the folk week-end was over Anna told her father it had been simply gorgeous and just what Madame had told her to do.

Peter had been to Scotland for his holiday. There was no folk-dancing festival there, but there was miles of space where he could dance with only the birds to watch him. One day he was taken to watch some Highland games and there he saw reels danced. For the rest of his holiday he tried to dance reels as the Highlanders did. He was not very successful.

Madame came back to the school as refreshed as if she had been away for years instead of for five weeks.

'I hope you've all had a wonderful dancing holiday,' she said. 'I have never enjoyed myself more. I have been to America, to a dancing teachers' conference. This included watching a lot of most exciting dancing. On Saturday I will tell you about it.'

Peter had been picked for his school football team. They played matches or had practice on Saturday afternoons, so he was able to continue meeting Anna at the bus stop and go with her to the Saturday morning class, as he had in the summer term.

That next Saturday, after the work-out session followed by folk dancing, Madame as usual told the children to sit on the floor.

'For the last two terms I have been showing you how dancing developed from the natural dancing of the people to the refinement of court dancing. How, through the efforts of Catherine de Medici who married a king of France, Paris became the headquarters of the dance. How Louis XIV sponsored the first ballet school and how, from dancer to dancer, technique and knowledge were passed on from generation to generation. We finished last term when, in the year 1847, Marius Petipa, a Frenchman, went to Russia which, with his help, was shortly to become the centre of the ballet world.

Square dancing in nineteenth-century America

'Although we now have an accepted dancing technique, every country has used this technique in her own way. Nowhere is this more true than in North America. The early settlers brought with them the folk dances of the European countries they had left behind. But, of course, conditions were different in the "new world". Only brave, independent people would have crossed the wild Atlantic and travelled hundreds of miles by wagon to settle in new homes. But they had now much more room and much more vigour, and this showed when they danced.

'I wish you could have been with me to see the crowd of all ages who came together to dance. What they danced most often was particularly their own. It is called square dancing. Each dance is run by a caller who is something like a conductor, for he calls to the dancers to tell them what to do next, often in very amusing rhyme. As well, I saw various versions of the running set I have taught you. That was discovered in Kentucky, but it belongs also, as I saw, to many neighbour States. All the country dancing that I watched had a splendid verve and a pep that is particularly North American.

'Because it was summer, the ballet companies were not dancing in New York, but I picked up on some dancers in summer-season musicals. In these there was little if any real ballet, but all the dancers had been trained for the ballet.

'I believe North American dancers bring to their art something that we in Western Europe have either forgotten or never known. There is of course their negro heritage. The millions of negro slaves, imported into North America to work on the Southern plantations, kept their spirits alive by their songs and their dances.

'In the nineteenth century the negro shuffle swept across the world; white audiences were delighted by the gaiety and laughter of negro dancers.

'Then, at the turn of the century, came the birth of jazz, and with it a new style of dancing rich in the negro's brilliant technique and rhythm. The veil of the fun-loving laughing negro was to be torn away to show the tragedy beneath. In the negro ballet company created by the dancer Katherine Dunham, classical ballet and the negro heritage were united.

'As we move on in our history, you will find North Americans playing an increasing part in it. When you get a chance to watch them dance, think of their immigrant forefathers who taught them to use space and freedom, look for their pep, and remember the American negros.'

CHAPTER EIGHT

The Tales of Beatrix Potter

All learning seems to creep up on you. Once letters were a complete mystery, then they became words, then a treasure was yours for ever. You could read.

Anna and Peter discovered dancing was like that. You worked away at the *barre* or in the centre struggling with your turn-out and watching your position in the long looking-glasses. Then one day you were taught something new, it was called an *enchaînement*. This was a string of steps—a dancing conversion. Then, not perhaps well, still full of faults, you were beginning to dance.

It was at this time that Madame brought some little books to her classes.

'I hope,' she told the children, 'you were all brought up on the books of Beatrix Potter. If you were not you should have been, for in their little way they are as much your birthright as the plays of William Shakespeare. There are twenty-three of her Tales here, but the ones I want you to read very carefully are *The Tale of Jemima Puddle-Duck*, *The Tale of Pigling Bland*, *The Tale of Jeremy Fisher*, *The Tale of Two Bad Mice* and *The Tale of Squirrel Nutkin*. You should also read *The Tale of Peter Rabbit* and *The Tale of Mrs Tiggy-Winkle*. You will find it extraordinary—I could scarcely believe it myself— but these five little stories have been woven into a ballet, danced by the Royal Ballet Company. I was afraid you had missed seeing it, but I am thankful to say it will be showing in this town next Christmas, and I would like to prepare you so that you can appreciate what is, I believe, a truly memorable achievement.'

Madame went on to tell the children a little about the life of Beatrix Potter. 'She was born in 1866 in London. At that date children of what were called the upper middle classes, which meant having nothing to do with trade, were mostly comfortably off or even rich. If Beatrix had known any other children they would have belonged to exactly the same background as herself. There was great belief in those days in what was called "knowing your place".

Julie Wood and Keith Martin as Mrs Tittlemouse and Johnny Town-Mouse in The Tales of Beatrix Potter

'Poor little Beatrix's place was to be alone in first the nursery and then the schoolroom. When she was five she did have a baby brother, but by the time he was old enough to play with her he was packed off to a boarding-school.

'But Beatrix's young life wasn't too grim. She was lucky in her governess, a woman of great delicacy of spirit who encouraged the child's awakening interest in nature and drawing. Beatrix Potter once said that she was thankful she had never been sent to school as "it would have rubbed off some of the originality". Perhaps it would have done. Perhaps with a wider life and friends of her own age she would never have written the Tales, but personally I doubt

it. Creative talent is born and not bred. If it is there it will choose its moment to flower.

'The choreographer of the film *The Tales of Beatrix Potter* was the great Sir Frederick Ashton himself and he danced Mrs Tiggy-Winkle. Just imagine what work Sir Frederick had undertaken! All of you, especially you boys, have learnt a little about the art of miming. So you can see how important miming must be to a film where not one word is spoken. Everything must be said through dancing and the movement of paws and head. But no faces, remember, for each dancer's face was hidden under a mask. Each movement, however tiny, had to be the right movement for the particular animal.

'The masks were made in three stages. The first, copying Beatrix Potter's illustrations exactly, a craftsman carved out the heads. The next stage was casting the heads. This is an expression which is used by sculptors and means having a head "cast" in plaster of Paris. But, of course, plaster of Paris would be too heavy for dancers to wear so instead very light plastic was used.

'At this stage a new problem had to be faced. How were the dancers to breathe? This was managed by making invisible little holes in the cheeks and snouts. At the same time some of the holes had to be big enough for the dancers to see through for the eyes in the masks were nowhere near the eyes of the dancers.

'The last stage was to dress the masks. This meant covering each head with fur or feathers. Also, of course, there were eyes and noses. For the squirrels who, as you know from Beatrix Potter's pictures, were not dressed in clothes, hairs—ten at a time—were stuck on to nylon frills. It took perhaps five thousand bunches of hair to make the skin of one squirrel.'

The children gasped.

'It must have taken ages,' Peter said.

'Ages to prepare,' Madame agreed, 'but just five weeks to make the film. A work of love. When Christmas comes, you will see for yourselves that *The Tales of Beatrix Potter* is a film of which the makers one and all can be proud.'

Coming home on the bus Peter said to Anna: 'I've read the Peter Rabbit books. We've got most of them. What I don't see is how they could make a film. I mean how could you mime in a mask?'

'Perhaps it's done like Donald Duck,' Anna suggested.

'It can't be,' Peter reminded her. 'Madame said it was danced by the Royal Ballet Company.'

Above: a sketch of the costume design for a squirrel in the Beatrix Potter film

Left: the Mouse-Waltz from the Beatrix Potter film

That term Peter was very involved in mime. With Eduardo they were learning a little about the ballet *Petrouchka*. Peter told Anna about it.

'Eduardo says he thinks it's the best ballet there is, but it isn't often danced. The reason is that it wants an awful lot of old dancers which most companies don't have. He says in Russia when dancers retire they are given pensions, then when old dancers are wanted they can be easily found.'

'Why does *Petrouchka* want old dancers?' Anna asked.

'Because it happens at a fair. It's a real fair, which there really was in Leningrad—only then it was St Petersburg—before Lent. Eduardo showed us some of the people at the fair: a coachman and a stall holder and a nursery maid, and the father with his family. He was very funny. But you could see ordinary thin dancers would look wrong for lots of the characters need to be fat.'

'What's *Petrouchka* about?' Anna wanted to know.

Peter tried to remember exactly what Eduardo had said.

'There are these puppets, you know, who seem real like Basil Brush, but aren't really. One is a girl who is a dancer, then there is Petrouchka and as well a black one called the Moor.'

'What do they do at the fair?' Anna asked.

'Dances, you know, like puppets do. But then you see them in their little rooms. Eduardo says the old showman is cruel to them. I don't know how you can be cruel to a puppet, but Eduardo says that Petrouchka has just the beginning of a soul. Anyway, Petrouchka, who is a sort of clown, loves the dancer, but the Moor, who is a beast and a show-off, takes her from him. In the end Petrouchka runs out into the snow where the Moor kills him with a scimitar, which is a kind of knife. All the people at the fair think they have seen a murder and fetch a policeman, but of course the showman lets them see Petrouchka is only a puppet. At least that's what he thinks, but at that minute a terrible cry is heard, and there, above the little theatre where the puppets work, are the head and shoulders of Petrouchka. Eduardo said this proved he had a soul.'

'*Petrouchka* sounds very sad,' said Anna.

Peter nodded. 'But Eduardo says it's perfect with gorgeous music by Stravinsky. I do wish I could see it danced.'

Petrouchka—a drawing by Gyula Hincz

70

CHAPTER NINE

Famous Dancers of Yesterday

One Saturday Madame told the class some more ballet history.

'You remember last term we left our ballet history in the year 1847 when Marius Petipa left Paris to dance in Russia. It was, I told you, only intended as a short visit, but he became chief choreographer so he stayed in St Petersburg for the rest of his life. While Petipa lived and worked in St Petersburg a remarkable change came over the ballet scene in Russia. There ballet came to have great prestige unheard of anywhere else in Europe where it was still the poor relation of the arts. In Russia the ballet was in fact rated as of the same importance as opera. Ballet, together with the great ballet schools, came under the direct control of the Imperial Household for in those days Russia was ruled by an emperor.

'*Theatre Street* is a classic book about the Maryinsky school in St Petersburg. It is written by the great star Tamara Karsavina who, as I shall be telling you, was to become a vital link between dancing as performed in Russia and dancing in the rest of the world. It tells in minute detail what it was like to be a pupil of a Russian ballet school at the turn of the century. Mind you, though this is only guesswork for I have never put a foot in a Russian ballet school, I believe in some ways they are run in the same way today.

'Slightly older than Tamara Karsavina was a dancer of whom you all must have heard. Anna Pavlova. She had, as far as is known, no dancing history behind her. Her mother was a washerwoman but nobody knows who her father was. She was a frail, delicate-looking child but always she must have had a will of iron. Pavlova's star quality was at once accepted by those in authority. Like Karsavina, she also danced for Diaghilev, but she left him after one season to begin what she was to do all her life—tour the world.

'There are no words to tell what Pavlova meant to the world. She awoke in countless thousands a love of dancing. She had exquisite feet and legs, in fact her feet are said to have been the most beautiful in ballet history. Pavlova's dancing career seems to have

Anna Pavlova in her rôle as the Dying Swan

73

been more like the passing of a comet than of a dancer. A comet moves across the sky rare and mysterious. I think Pavlova must have been like that. Brought up in a Russian ballet school, she was nurtured on the great ballets but she scarcely ever danced them. She trained her own ballet company of, most surprisingly, English girls —for nobody at that time thought English girls could dance. Two or three of those girls are still teaching today. Pavlova had in her time five different leading male soloists to partner her. The choreography, the designs, the music of almost all her ballets were perhaps second-rate, but none of this mattered. She had a magic no one could touch and her name will mean dancing until the world ends. Incidentally she did perform one classical ballet. A tiny solo called *The Dying Swan*, choreographed by Fokine. It is seldom danced now for it so definitely belonged to Pavlova; it still seems, to many dancers, sacrilege to attempt to dance it.

'One bad thing came out of Pavlova's meteoric career which especially affected North America. She left behind in each town where she had danced a trail of children crying out that they too must dance. Not only were there not enough trained teachers for all these children, but it encouraged teachers to teach who had not been properly trained, sometimes not trained at all. As a result, behind Pavlova there were a collection of maimed feet and, in some cases, broken bodies, not to mention broken hearts, for one thing is certain—those who teach ballet must be very thoroughly trained themselves or lasting harm will be done.

'Now I must remind you about another dancer who belonged to the Pavlova period. This was the male dancer I mentioned in connection with *Spectre de la Rose*, the dancer called Nijinsky. He too was trained at the Maryinsky school and became a star member of the Maryinsky company until Diaghilev engaged him as his leading male dancer for his first great season in Paris. I never saw Nijinsky dance but Eduardo did and has, I expect, talked to you boys about him.' All the boys nodded, for Nijinsky was one of Eduardo's heroes and there was seldom a class when he was not mentioned.

Madame went on. 'He was a beautiful dancer, what the Russians called a "*danseur noble*", but the gift for which he is always remembered was jumping or, more technically, *élévation*. According to those who saw him, he could jump higher than any dancer had before; he jumped like a flying bird and at the top of his flight he paused in the air before he came down. You all know what an *entrechat* is—a crossing of the legs in mid-air. Well Nijinsky could

Right: sketches made in 1913 of some dance movements and the corresponding music for Le Sacre du Printemps (The Rite of Spring)—*the music is by Stravinsky and the original 1913 version was choreographed by Nijinsky and performed by Diaghilev's Ballets Russes*

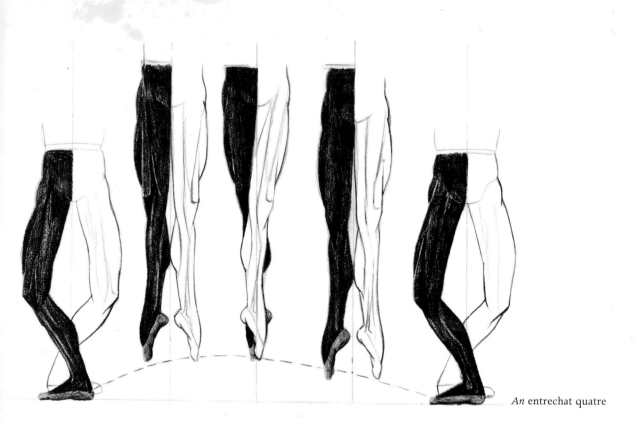

An entrechat quatre

perform an *entrechat douze*; that is to say he made twelve movements in mid-air—second and fifth position alternately—closing the fifth position each time with a *battement*. Then he paused. At least all ballet historians say he did and we must believe them. But whether he did or not does not really matter; he had the magic to make his audiences believe that he did and that is true magic.

'All the way through the history of ballet individualists have sprung up. People who believed passionately in the art of dancing, but not always in the technique of ballet. I am going to tell you a little about two of these. The first was Isadora Duncan. She was an American from San Francisco. She was born in 1878, and died in 1927. This means that at the time of her birth the ballet centre of the world had already moved to Russia. Ballet technique was clearly defined. Ballet shoes though darned, as indeed they are today, were already stiffened when bought, though how much stiffened depended, and depends today, on individual dancers. The ballet hierarchy was clearly defined—unless you were exceptionally gifted you started your career in the *corps de ballet*; then, if you were successful, you moved on to become a *coryphée*. *Coryphées* are a

76

group half-way between the *corps de ballet* and the soloists. Usually they dance in groups of six or eight. Next come the soloists, then, finally, the *ballerinas* who occasionally rise to be *prima ballerinas*. Into this ordered world sprang Isadora Duncan, a girl who believed movement should be unhampered by corsets or indeed by clothes. For a brief Greek tunic seems to have been all that she felt needed to be worn; her feet were usually bare. To me, trained in the strict formalized world of the ballet, it is hard to believe I should have cared to watch Isadora Duncan, but others far more knowledgeable than myself insist she was an important torch bearer in her day. She was a liberator. A believer in free movement, she influenced thinking. For many she turned the world upside down. She was inspired by great music. Everybody should dance to it; dancing was using your body as it was meant to be used to express the glory of being alive, even the glory of God.

'Isadora Duncan died before she was fifty in a car accident. After her death, and indeed during her lifetime, imitators sprang up. That is the worst about people like Duncan. Their ideas may be good but, because they lack technique, they are fatally easy to copy. However, Duncan influenced one person who was of the utmost importance to ballet. This was the great choreographer Fokine. I shall be telling you about him when we think about the stories of the ballets.

'There were so many imitators of Duncan, quite a number of whom made names for themselves, that I shan't confuse you by telling you about them, but there is one dancer that I must mention. Her name is Martha Graham. She, like Duncan, belonged to America. She too, like Duncan, had no belief in the old classical ballets. She invented her own dance steps and movements, usually using her limbs and muscles in the opposite way you are being taught to use yours. She was and is, for she is still alive, enormously serious about her work. Each dance that she has choreographed has had something which to her was of vital importance to say. And, as if she were a magnet, she gathered to her very intelligent people of all nationalities, who were prepared to spend their lives learning to teach their bodies to say what she wanted them to say. Martha Graham's name will live and others will carry on where she has left off. Many of her ballets are very beautiful though very difficult. But if some day you get a chance to see a Martha Graham ballet, go. It's a memorable experience.'

Madame got up. 'One Saturday soon I shall be telling you about some of the great dancers of today.'

CHAPTER TEN

Ulanova

That autumn three girls dropped out of Anna's class and four boys out of Peter's. Of course both Anna and Peter knew the children who had left for they had talked to them in the changing room, but they could not remember anyone saying that they were giving up.

One Saturday Peter said to Anna as they were riding home on the bus from their morning class, 'I suppose if Madame or Eduardo doesn't think somebody is doing all right they might tell them so. I mean, one way and another it costs quite a lot to learn.'

'I know that girl called Doris who has left was sick of being told about her posture, and that one called Sybil told me her father said she could have riding lessons instead of coming to dancing but she couldn't have both.'

'Do you ever think about giving it up?' Peter asked Anna.

Anna looked at him in astonishment. 'Goodness no! I'd rather die. Would you give it up?'

Peter took quite a time to answer. 'It's games. I don't want to swank, but at school they think I might do well. My father played cricket and rugger for his university. I know what he would like is that I do the same.'

Anna just couldn't understand. Imagine anyone giving up dancing just to play games!

'But wouldn't you miss dancing?'

'Course, but it's going to be a bit of a pull in two years' time. That's when I'll move into another school. You see, if I'm to get a place in a university I'll have to work like stink. It's much more difficult now to get a place than when Dad got in.'

'Will your father make you give up dancing?'

Peter shook his head. 'Oh no! Dad would never do that. He'll only advise if I ask him. But I should think he might go to Madame and Eduardo and see what they say.'

'And what d'you suppose they'll say?'

Peter looked Anna straight in the eyes. 'If I tell you something, will you absolutely swear not to tell anybody else?'

'Of course.'

Galina Ulanova being lifted by her partner Nicolai Fadeyechev in rehearsal for Giselle

Peter lowered his voice so no one in the bus could hear. 'Eduardo told me that if I worked he thought Madame might let me try for a place in the senior school at the Royal Ballet, but I wasn't to tell anybody. Anyway of course that wouldn't happen for ages.'

Anna's eyes shone. 'How glorious if she did! I wish Madame would say that to me.'

Peter looked sympathetic. 'Eduardo says it's much more difficult for girls. Only one in thousands gets a chance.'

'Lucky you,' said Anna. 'I wish I'd been born a boy.'

Even though nobody said anything particularly encouraging that term Anna could see for herself that her work was improving. There was more centre practice and more *enchaînements*. She could perform quite neatly a series of *pirouettes*. With one hand on the *barre*

Boy in an arabesque *position*

80

she could manage a well-positioned *arabesque*. She did not and was not expected to raise the leg extended at the back very high, but the placing was right and she could feel when it was right. The *port de bras* exercises were becoming more difficult for she had to learn to use her arms at the same time as her feet, legs and body. Then there was stretching. Anna rather enjoyed this. It was always worked at just at the end of a class when the muscles were warmed up. It meant lifting one leg on to the *barre*, then carry on with the *port de bras* exercise while one hand held you in position at the *barre*. It looked good, Anna thought, and she hoped it was good.

Even though she was sure she was improving, Anna thought a lot about what Peter had said. Next year she too would be eleven. That would certainly mean that harder school work was on the way. There would be homework and some day O levels. Dad and Mum, especially Dad, would expect her to pass her exams. Probably they were already thinking about what she would do when she left school. One thing was certain, they were not thinking of her being a dancer. They were expecting her to have given it up long before she left school. Already her mother said things like: 'If it wasn't for that wretched Saturday morning dancing class you could be such a help to me, Anna. Why, you could do all the shopping,' or 'I wish you could cut a dancing class occasionally. You are going to miss such a lot of nice parties at Christmas.'

'I know inside me I won't give up,' Anna told Peter. 'I know it's almost impossible to get into a ballet company. But I'll be trained for ballet and that is a help for all dancing. I'm sure if I work hard Madame will tell me how you get to dance on TV and things like that.'

'The trouble is,' said Peter, 'it's not a thing that shows like playing the piano. Only you and me know how hard we work.'

Though, of course, the children did not know it, at that very minute Fate was helping them. Peter's father was visiting a patient who was also the vicar of his parish church.

'How's Peter's dancing coming along?' the vicar asked.

Peter's father put away his stethoscope. 'He never says much about it, but I'm afraid he's still keen. I'd like to see him give it up and concentrate on sport.'

The vicar looked sympathetic. 'Give him his head. No good will come of forcing him. As a matter of fact I was wondering if Peter could help me out at Christmas. There's a big party for my old people. I wondered if Peter would dance.'

The doctor disliked the idea but he didn't say so.

'You ask him. If he agrees it's OK with me.'

The vicar then heard that Anna learnt at the same dancing school. He asked Peter if he thought the two of them could dance together.

Peter told Anna about it. Her eyes grew enormous with excitement.

'We'll have to ask Madame but if she says "yes" then I'll talk to Mum. Imagine the glory if she said she'd make me a proper tutu!'

Anna's dreams of a tutu were doomed. Madame took Peter's request very calmly.

'Of course,' she agreed. 'You can dance the Irish jig I teach you on Saturdays. You both know it. Dancing it will be fun for you and fun for the old people. Don't forget to finish with a *révérence*.'

The next Saturday, after the class had danced the Irish jig, Madame as usual settled in her chair and the children sat on the floor.

'The history of dancing today is much the most difficult part of history to tell, for I have to pick the truly greats out of the milky way of stars of today. You must remember the choice is my choice. Other people who love dancing and know more about it may give you a different list, but I think all will agree about my first choice. She is retired now from dancing, but she still teaches. I am talking about Galina Ulanova.

'Ulanova is a truly superb artist. Early during the siege of Leningrad, the Russians, who look upon their great artists as they look upon their great works of art, evacuated her and other members of the company to Moscow, which is how Ulanova became a member of the Bolshoi Ballet company. I was lucky enough to see her dance in London. It was a most remarkable experience. I don't know what I had expected to see, but it certainly was not the Ulanova I saw. A not very young woman in a not particularly becoming white dress. Then a miracle. The orchestra played her music and, as I watched, she was fourteen and jumped on to her nurse's lap. From that second there was no Ulanova. She was Juliet. When Ulanova was training a young dancer to dance Giselle she told Mr Albert Kahn, who has produced a book about her, "I wanted to develop her imagination. Without that an artist has no being." Try and remember those words of Ulanova's all your lives, for if any of you should become a dancer when you grow up, or a writer, or a painter, or a musician, you must never forget that you will achieve nothing without imagination.'

Galina Ulanova rehearses Ekaterina Maximova for her debut as Giselle at the Bolshoi Theatre

CHAPTER ELEVEN

Dancing in Britain

The Irish jig was an immense success with the old people. Both Peter and Anna had by now good neat foot-work and, as they had danced the jig on many Saturdays, they knew it backwards. Added to this the vicar had provided not only a good pianist but a violin; it was wonderful how that violin put spring into their feet.

Of course Anna did not wear a tutu, but both Peter's mother and her mother had put their heads together, so they were dressed in the sort of fancy dress supposed once to have been worn by the Irish peasants. It was not correct but they looked charming and had to dance the jig twice.

Both mothers were at the entertainment and were proud of their children. When they got home they tried to make their husbands feel proud too but they were not very successful.

'She really can dance,' Anna's mother said. 'I can't explain it but it's there. Everybody said so.'

'You can think what you like,' Peter's mother told his father, 'but he was splendid. He looked every bit as manly as he would playing cricket.'

'Oh well,' said his father, 'I daresay a good athlete should be able to dance, but I hope he gives it up before it gets a hold on him.'

As a reward for having done so well at the old people's party the mothers bought Peter and Anna seats for *The Tales of Beatrix Potter*. They both planned to take great interest in the choreography, they meant to study the foot-work of the dancers, but somehow they never did. They did marvel at the scenery which reduced full-sized people to the size of mice. For days afterwards Peter tried to leap like Jeremy Fisher. But mostly the ballet sucked them into the stories. For that afternoon they were little animals of the farm and the hedgerow.

There was a very short Christmas holiday and then dancing classes started again. On the first Saturday of the term Madame started telling the children a little about the dancing scene in England.

Michael Coleman in the rôle of Jeremy Fisher in The Tales of Beatrix Potter

'Last term I told you about dancing in Russia and how she became the centre of the dancing world; and I told you a little about Diaghilev. Now this term we will start with Diaghilev.

'Diaghilev was a most unusual man. He was not a performer himself but a thinker, a dreamer and, in his way, a revolutionary. In Russia he had become disgusted with officialdom as it affected the arts. Soon he had formed a group of artists who felt the need to break away, to find freedom and to express new views. The art they chose through which to express themselves was ballet. It could and should say everything they wanted to say. I am not going to confuse you with the names of the great who gathered together: artists to design the scenery and clothes, story-tellers, choreographers and, of course, dancers. There are literally dozens of books about Diaghilev and his times, all written by people more competent than I am to tell the story—some indeed danced in his company.

'At the time when Diaghilev was building his first company, dancing outside Russia was in the doldrums. There were good dancers about but few to produce them, and they were badly treated. Paris, once as you know the centre of the ballet world, showed ballets only on the nights when opera did not want the stage, and the male dancers were scarcely used at all.

'In London ballet was only popular as a turn in the music-hall programmes. It flourished in London, particularly at a theatre called the Empire.

'I believe it is impossible for us today to realize what the Diaghilev ballet meant to the public in that first season, which was in 1909. As choreographer Diaghilev had chosen the best in the world—Michel Fokine.

'Fokine, too, was a revolutionary. He had for a long time been dissatisfied with ballet as it was in Russia. He had been made restless by Isadora Duncan. He wanted each ballet to be a work of art. Exquisite music on which to plan every step of the ballet. Imaginative scenery, not necessarily elaborate but catching exactly the mood of the ballet. Finally, of course, the best dancers.

'At that moment in time it was possible for Diaghilev to get the best dancers. To dance abroad for a season was customary; the season over the dancers could return to Russia. But this system came to an end with the Russian Revolution. Then Diaghilev was out of Russia, few Russian dancers could get out and, if they got out, they could not get back. Diaghilev had to look elsewhere for his dancers.

86

Isadora Duncan, a contemporary impression by Bourdelle

'There was so much Diaghilev gave the world it is hard not to exaggerate, but I must mention colour. Ballet had been what we should now call pretty-pretty. Delicate pinks and blues, with frilly skirts and ribbon bows. Diaghilev gave the world colour, violent colours, if necessary clashing colours. Not, of course, in all ballets, still some called for white and in *Spectre de la Rose* the dancers wore dresses much the same as you saw today's dancers wear. But colour was part of Diaghilev's gift to the world, and quite literally he changed the way people lived. The greeny-yellow look vanished and into the most unlikely homes came scarlet curtains and piles of vivid cushions. It was the same with clothes; during Diaghilev's day nothing was too bright to wear; they were right, bright clothes make you feel gay and look gay.

Following page: Rudolph Nureyev and Margot Fonteyn in Marguerite and Armand, *a ballet created for these two artists by Frederick Ashton*

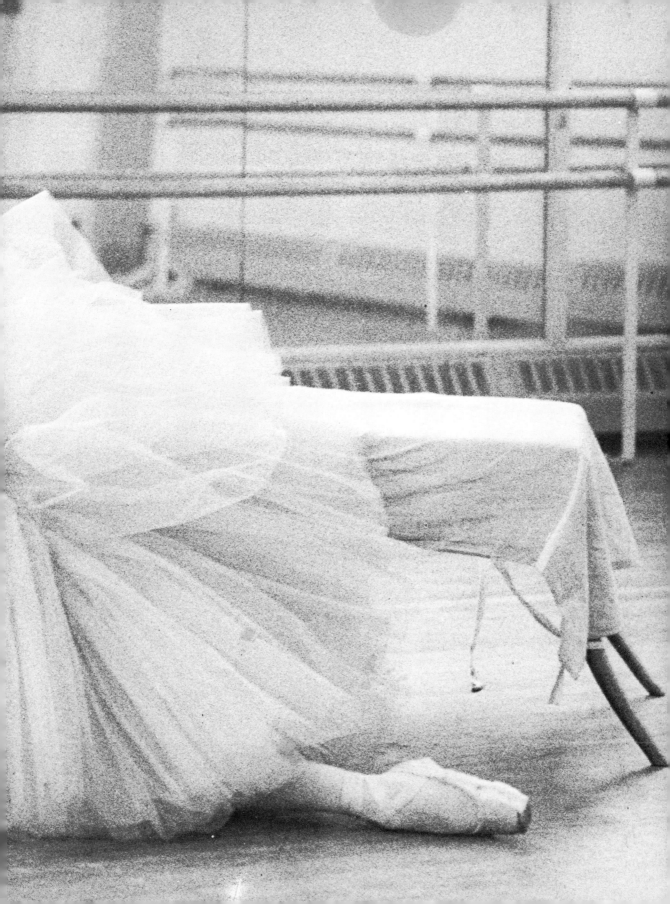

'After the First World War and the Russian Revolution, in the year 1923, Diaghilev engaged an English girl to dance in his company. She called herself Ninette de Valois but her real name was Edris Stanners. She came from Ireland. With Diaghilev she rose to be a soloist, but she left him in 1925 to establish a ballet school in London. Not that he let her go altogether for when she could she still danced for him for a season.

'It is far too long a story to tell you now but for all who are interested I recommend Dame Ninette de Valois's own book, *Come Dance with Me*. In this book, you will learn of the extraordinary achievement of this young woman, as she was then. England at the time had no ballet of her own. There was and is a company trained by a marvellous woman called Marie Rambert; she has now been made a Dame. There was a society called the Camargo Society, which kept ballet alive by performances largely danced on Sundays, and there was Ninette de Valois and pupils trained at her school. Then —and this is the long story I am leaving out—after six years English ballet was born.

'There was at that time a great figure in the theatre. Her name was Lilian Baylis but those who knew and worked for her just called her "The Lady". Ninette de Valois pleaded with Miss Baylis to provide her with a theatre for her dancers and room for a school; she gave all she had to give of her own to the enterprise: her money—and this included her earnings; her talent—and do not forget she had been a soloist for Diaghilev; almost her life, for the energy she poured out on the new theatre was enormous. Anyway, thanks to these two remarkable women, Lilian Baylis and Ninette de Valois, in 1931, at the Sadler's Wells Theatre, the Vic-Wells Ballet was born.

'It was a mercy that Ninette de Valois had her company fairly well established before the Second World War started. Those were terrible years for ballet. All the male dancers who were of the right age were called up to serve in the Forces. Long periods of what the army calls "square bashing", which really means drilling, is the last thing a dancer needs, nor does it help him to man a gun in the Navy or learn to fly a plane. The company who were left had to dance without an orchestra for years, managing with two pianos. In 1940 the company were sent to tour Holland and they were there when Holland was invaded. They did escape on a cargo boat, but lost much of their wardrobe, scenery and music. How the ballet struggled on to final triumphs is now history, which I shall leave you to discover for yourselves.

Dame Ninette de Valois and Sir Frederick Ashton watching a rehearsal at the Royal Ballet School

91

'Now here are some of the dancers you should know about who helped to build our national ballet.

'Markova was a child pupil of Marie Rambert. Then one day Diaghilev came to the Rambert studio, saw her dance, and invited her to join his company. Ninette de Valois, remembering those days in her book, writes, ''There was Markova, this tiny prim little girl . . .''. Markova was British—her real name was Alice Marks—and she was accompanied by a good British governess. I have often thought the shy little English girl aged fourteen and her governess must have looked oddly out of place beside the glittering members of the Diaghilev ballet. But Diaghilev had a great eye for talent and he had tremendous plans for his little English girl. Then suddenly he was dead and all his dancers must have felt as if they had come up against a brick wall. They had literally no future—nowhere to dance. Perhaps no one was more crushed than Markova for, at the end of his last season, Diaghilev had told her he was revising a ballet called *Giselle*—which I shall be telling you about—and she was to dance Giselle.

'However, Diaghilev was right about Markova's talent and she was soon to appear again. This time as star dancer with the Sadler's Wells Theatre ballet, together with a brilliant male dancer called Anton Dolin. But Markova and Dolin were world stars and soon moved on. The Vic-Wells then found their own leading dancer—a foreign-looking child who had been trained in the Sadler's Wells school. Her real name was Peggy Hookham but she was soon to emerge, the pride of the British ballet world, as Margot Fonteyn.'

The children all settled down with a sort of pleased sigh. To have reached Margot Fonteyn was like driving home after being a long time away. Here was somebody they had heard of ever since they could remember. Somebody they felt they knew.

Madame paused and the children knew she was seeing something in her memory. Something beautiful, for her face looked radiant. Then she said, 'I wish so much it was in my power to show you children some of the great dancers I have seen. Margot Fonteyn was one of the greatest. It is not possible to describe great dancing, but when you see it you recognize it with your whole body. It is perfection, a oneness between the dancer and the music.'

Madame got up. 'Now we'll have a final go at that running set before you go home.'

Margot Fonteyn in La Bayadère

92

CHAPTER TWELVE

A Problem

Madame had to be away for two Saturdays judging some dancing examinations, so Eduardo took her classes. They heard no ballet history from him but he was very interesting about the Beatrix Potter film. He showed them with surprising delicacy how different-ly a mouse danced to a pig. At the end he pretended to be Mrs Tiggy-Winkle and somehow he was just like her.

The last Saturday of the term Madame came back to her history of ballet.

'The last time I spoke to you about ballet history, I was talking about Margot Fonteyn.

'The next star I must tell you about is a man. He is called Robert Helpmann. Helpmann joined the English ballet from Australia. He came over entirely on chance with just a letter of introduction. It took Ninette de Valois no time to realize she had a find; probably it took her longer to persuade Lilian Baylis to put him under contract, but she succeeded.

'Robert Helpmann is a truly great mime but he is also a great actor. He was provided by God with the most remarkable face, with huge goggling eyes. That face tells everything. But he has a perfectly trained body of which every bit can and does act. He is also a fine choreographer.

'When he was dancing regularly with the company it was my holiday treat to go and watch him and, though he has made me laugh so much it has hurt, I think I have gained even more from his tragedies. What an artist!

'I have already told you a little about Frederick Ashton. He is probably the most prolific choreographer of modern times. He was born in South America, in a place called Guayaquil in Ecuador. He arrived in London when he was eighteen determined to become a dancer. He became a pupil of, amongst others, Massine, a dancer of immense talent and importance to ballet history whom we shall come to in a minute.

'Frederick Ashton—now "Sir"—has always been enormously

Comic miming at its best, with Frederick Ashton and Robert Helpmann as the Ugly Sisters in Cinderella

successful both as a dancer and as a choreographer. He is also enormously funny; I cannot describe to you his performance together with Robert Helpmann as the ugly sisters in *Cinderella*. I ached I laughed so much.

'Then there is Michael Somes who comes from the West Country and was Margot Fonteyn's principal partner in the fifties.

'There was, of course, a galaxy of girl dancers who helped to build British ballet. Red-headed Moira Shearer, who was a lovely dancer as well as making her name in the film *The Red Shoes*. Svetlana Beriosova, a Lithuanian who joined the Royal Ballet, as the original Vic-Wells Ballet has now become, by way of Canada and Monte Carlo. Nadia Nerina from South Africa, Beryl Grey of England. I could go on giving you names for hours. Then there are stars of the moment: Antoinette Sibley, Monica Mason, Doreen Wells, Merle Park from South Africa, and Lynne Seymour. Amongst the men dancers are Anthony Dowell, Alexander Grant and half a dozen more, but I think the greatest favourite is the Russian who at one time joined the Royal Ballet company. I mean of course Nureyev.

'Nureyev, when he joined the Royal Ballet, for a while partnered Margot Fonteyn. Although they are many years apart in age, they dance exquisitely together; to watch them is an experience I shall always remember. Nureyev is a special sort of Russian called a Tartar. It's been a great thing for British ballet having Nureyev to work with. He has left us now to be what is called a freelance dancer, which means he can dance where he likes. Fortunately he still visits us as a guest artist. Apart from the fact that he is a great dancer, he brings qualities to his dancing that no British dancer possesses. He has fire inherited from his Tartar ancestors. He is stunningly acrobatic. When he dances at his best you can almost see a flame lighting inside him which illuminates his whole performance. I will tell you one extra thing about Nureyev. He comes from a remote, desperately poor village; as a child he knew what it was to be hungry. Yet look at him now. Which just shows if you have the talent it can carry you to the top however hard your beginnings.

'I told you I would tell you about Leonide Massine. He has been a great figure in dancing from the days of Diaghilev. For Nijinsky left Diaghilev very suddenly and Diaghilev, looking for someone to take his place, discovered Massine at the State dancing school in what was then St Petersburg. Massine was seventeen.

'Diaghilev, as I have said before, was a miraculous talent-spotter.

Doreen Wells in Romeo and Juliet

He saw at once the vast possibilities in the boy with the huge expressive eyes. By 1915 Massine was a leading dancer in the Diaghilev company and its choreographer. What a start! Sometimes I say to Eduardo, ''Have you found me a Massine yet?'' But he only sighs and says, ''We must not expect more than one Massine in a century.''

'After the war he left Diaghilev for some years and made his name in the revue world, dancing in one of C. B. Cochran's revues *On with the Dance*. Your grandmothers will tell you about C. B. Cochran who was a great figure in his day.

'After Diaghilev's death in 1929, Massine joined a company called after its founder, Colonel de Basil, and created for him a number of famous ballets. But he is best known for two he produced for Diaghilev—*La Boutique Fantasque* and *Le Tricorne*. This last had a décor by Picasso. Massine, of course danced in these ballets himself, and was a riot in a Spanish dance he invented called the Facucca.'

It was only a few weeks after Madame had told the children about Massine that she made her usual joke to Eduardo: 'Found me a Massine yet?' But this time Eduardo did not shake his head.

'Not a Massine but I am not sure we have not found a star in the

Some examples of élévation—*above:* sissone à la seconde; *below right:* cabriole derrière

98

making. He can dance a fine *entrechat six* and he has the makings of a good mime.'

'Is it Peter we are talking about?' Madame asked.

'Yes. I think perhaps he should try for a scholarship at the Royal Ballet School.'

Madame hesitated as if wondering how much to say.

'I know what you mean about Peter. He ought certainly to be given every chance, but I'm afraid if I tell his parents what I think they will simply remove him from the school. I don't think his father can be made to believe dancing is for men.'

'So we do nothing?' Eduardo asked.

'Let me think,' Madame said. 'Perhaps I will see a way. But I don't hold out much hope. His father was very athletic—he made a name for himself in sport at his university. I feel sure he wants Peter to do the same.'

'It will be a great waste if he does not use his talent,' said Eduardo. 'It is a pity he is born British. If he was Russian it would be a different story.'

Madame nodded.

'We must hope,' she said.

CHAPTER THIRTEEN

To Be Eleven

The summer term felt different from other terms. That autumn both Peter and Anna would be eleven. It would be the beginning of harder school work but if Madame had her way it would also be the beginning of harder dancing training too.

'Is your mother ever in town?' she asked Anna. 'I would like a word with her. You ought to come to me for an extra class next term.'

Anna knew her mother felt better about her dancing classes since she had watched her dance the Irish jig, but that did not mean she would like her going for an extra class.

'Mum doesn't often get time to come in. You see, the little ones have to be fetched from school.'

Madame had expected this. 'I'm afraid I must ask her to get you a leotard and some blocked shoes.'

Anna flushed with pleasure. To all dance students the first blocked shoes are an event.

'I'm sure she'll buy those. She knows I have to have them. But I'll wait for a good moment to ask her about the extra class.'

'I should like you to come to the Friday class as well as Tuesday's and Thursday's,' Madame explained. 'But I really would rather talk this over with your mother. Do try to persuade her to come and see me.'

To Peter Madame said nothing. She was making a secret plan to talk to his father.

The next Saturday Madame talked about dancing in America.

'Don't think,' she said, 'that I have held back on North America because it is not part of the general picture of ballet. It is a part and a very important part because ballet belongs to the world. I told you about the particular style which is notably American. I told you a little about Martha Graham and I have quoted the teachings of that brilliant choreographer Agnes de Mille, but now we are going to look at the general American picture.

'Go back a bit and think over what I have told you and you will

Martha Graham dancing in Ted Shawn's Aztec ballet Xochitl *in 1922*

remember the enormous influence of Pavlova who showed millions of Americans a new world. But of course America was not ready for thousands of children all saying ''I must learn to dance, I just must''. So for a short while many, many dancers in the making fell by the way. But the condition was not allowed to last and soon pianos were thumping, dancing slippers were being bought and most of North America's talent was learning to dance.

'Unlike most European countries and all towns in the Soviet Union, America has no State-sponsored ballet companies. Millions have been poured into ballet by private donors, but there is no State-sponsored ballet company and no State-sponsored school. You might think that this means the torch of dancing was not picked up in America, that Americans did not accept the technique patiently built up over the years. But I believe you would be wrong. What I imagine has happened is that the great American dancers have learnt for eight or nine years the full accepted ballet technique and then, when occasion has allowed, adapted it to what I can only call American dancing. This is appallingly hard work because in many cases it means using the muscles in exactly the opposite way than they were trained to be used. But the great gift that American dancing has given the world is that they have made dancing a contemporary art. It is no longer necessary to go to watch a ballet to see great dancing, it is part of the entertainment of the people, as much a part of the American way of life as blueberry pie.

'I do wish you had been old enough to see the great period of American musicals. *Oklahoma* literally left me breathless. One small ballet danced by a group of girls was not just exquisite to watch—it was so elegant. Then later we had *West Side Story*; this is really all ballet with words and songs added. There have been, too, some wonderful small ballets. I can still remember the thrill with which I first saw *Fancy Free*. This was one of the early examples of American dancing. The sailors, though dancing a difficult ballet, never made one move a sailor would not make.

'This is not to suggest you cannot see the old ballets danced in the USA; of course you can, perfectly danced. But the choreographers have been and are finding an American way to use the body.

'Before I leave the subject of dancing in the USA, I must explain why we see so little of it over here. The answer is money. Just imagine what it costs to transport enough scenery and clothes for, say, twenty ballets. The leading players of the orchestra or even the entire orchestra. All the music, all the instruments. Then there are

Following page: pupils at the ballet school of the Paris Opera practising arm movements

those who run the different departments. The wardrobe mistress and her staff. The managerial staff, the leading stage hands and, of course, the whole ballet company. The cost of moving a ballet company about is enormous. It is good for us all to think about these things; there is nothing airy-fairy about the bones of ballet, they are made of slogging hard work, money and, of course, talent.'

It was the Saturday that Madame had talked about America that the telegram came to Anna's father. Anna was busy at the time getting her homework done before she went to tea with Peter, so she did not hear about it. When she did hear it did not mean a great deal to her at the time. As so often happens, what is going to change your whole life seems for the moment to slither by.

It was when she came in from tea with Peter that her mother said, 'Dad's got to go to Scotland. Gran has died. He got a telegram this afternoon.'

Anna had never known her Gran well. When her grandfather had died she had sold the farm they had lived on and gone to live in a tiny cottage with no room for visitors. So Anna just said she was sorry and went upstairs to get ready for supper.

It was when her father came back from the funeral that all the whispering began. Then one day Dad and Mum told her their plans. Dad was going to sell their present house and move to some property that had belonged to Gran.

'It's just the place for a vet,' Dad said, 'nothing but farms for miles.'

Anna felt as if she had swallowed a piece of ice. She licked her lips.

'What about my dancing classes?' she whispered. Her full voice would not come out properly.

Dad knew it was no good beating about the bush. 'I'm afraid you'll have to forget about those. There won't be a dancing school within miles.'

*Frederick Ashton rehearsing
Marilyn Trounson and Carl
Myers for Ashton's ballet*
Lament of the Waves

CHAPTER FOURTEEN

Stories of the Ballet

Of course Anna told Peter her news. He was very sorry she was moving but he did not believe there would be no dancing class.

'There must be a town somewhere near; there always is,' he protested. 'I should think you might have to go to classes less often, but there are bound to be buses and trains and things.'

Anna knew better. 'I have always heard Dad say Grand-dad lived at the other end of everywhere. He was a sheep farmer. That's why we're moving. It's nothing but farms round there, which is just right for a vet.'

Peter could see that Anna had convinced herself there would be no dancing classes, so he made a sensible suggestion. 'If I were you I'd tell Madame. I bet she'll know where you can learn.'

Anna was still scared of Madame, but she could see it was a good idea. So after her next class she stayed behind to speak to her.

Madame listened to Anna's tale of woe and in her mind's eye saw the part of the country where Anna was going to live. It certainly was not a good place for dancing classes. When Anna had finished she gave her a kiss.

'Cheer up, child. I am certain something will be arranged. Not perhaps work as you do it here, but you are going to the land of reels and a period of learning to dance those would do every dancer good.'

Madame was now telling her Saturday class the stories of some of the ballets.

'Not that they all have stories that can be written down. I would start with *La Fille Mal Gardée* because it is the oldest ballet still danced regularly, but most of you saw that performed, so all I shall say about it is that it was first danced in London in 1786. Now I want us to skip about one hundred years to look at some of the ballets given us by that most prolific choreographer—Michel Fokine. You boys have been learning a little about his wonderful ballet *Petrouchka* with Eduardo. It is so difficult to decide which ballet to choose when

Nadia Nerina as Lise in Frederick Ashton's La Fille Mal Gardée

110

there are so many to choose from. In the end I have decided on *The Firebird* because it is always being danced somewhere. The last time I saw it, Margot Fonteyn danced the bird. What a lovely performance she gave!

'*The Firebird* has music by Stravinsky. It starts with a superb overture which puts you straight away in a fairy-tale mood. When the curtain goes up the stage is in darkness except for the centre where a tree grows covered with glowing fruit. By degrees the light becomes stronger and then the audience sees a flame-coloured bird flit across the stage. Then a young man dressed for hunting climbs over a wall at the back of the stage. The flame-coloured bird flies to the glowing fruit tree, whereupon the man raises his bow and arrow and tries to shoot her, but he misses. The young man, who is a prince, then chases the bird and in the end catches her. He lets her free in exchange for one of her gorgeous magic feathers.

'The stage is by now light enough for everything to be clear. Huge gates can be seen through which come twelve young girls who pick the golden apples off the tree to play with. But then the villain of the ballet arrives, he is called Köstchei. Köstchei tries to kill the prince but he is saved by his magic feather. Instead the prince kills Köstchei for he finds an enormous egg in which Köstchei's soul lives. This he smashes. It all ends happily for the prince gets engaged to the prettiest of the girls. The glorious firebird is left to enjoy her freedom and her wonderful golden fruit tree. This is a very bare outline of the ballet, for it has most exciting choreography and a terrifying collection of goblins and other evil creatures who attend on Köstchei. It was first danced by the Diaghilev company in Paris in 1910.

'As I have explained, many of the ballets don't have proper stories, just as operas very seldom tell stories like plays do. The obvious ones you can read for yourselves, such as *Cinderella, The Sleeping Princess, Romeo and Juliet* and *A Midsummer Night's Dream*. What I want to do is to tell you what I can about ballets there is a reasonable chance that you can see. No ballet company can keep more than a limited number of ballets in their repertoire at the same time. Just think of the scenery, the costumes, the orchestra and music, let alone the dancers. The miracle is they dance as many as they do, especially when on tour. Just think of *The Firebird* and imagine what it is like merely to be responsible for the clothes.

'Now I must tell you about one of Massine's ballets. It sounds simple and in a way it is, it is called *La Boutique Fantasque*. This is

Monica Mason in Kenneth MacMillan's version of The Rite of Spring

not a title which translates well but roughly it means the fantastic toyshop. This is exactly what it is about. It is bursting with gaiety and fun. It is in one act with music by Rossini. There is no story to tell but if ever you get a chance, be certain to go and see it. It is absolutely delightful.'

That day they finished the Saturday class by running through all the folk dances they now knew. Even while she was dancing Anna thought 'I bet this is the only sort of dancing I shall dance for ever and ever'.

Before the term finished Madame managed to see Peter's father. She heard there was a medical conference in the town, and she went to the hotel where it was being held and sent in her card to him with written on it: 'Could I see you for a minute?' Peter's father did not want to see Madame, but it just happened that her card arrived during a very boring speech so, looking as if he was answering a medical call, he slipped out.

Madame wasted no time. 'I think, and so does Eduardo who teaches my boys, that Peter may have a most successful future as a dancer.' She saw revulsion on the doctor's face, so she hurried on. 'We may be wrong but I do beg you to consider giving the boy his chance.'

'Well, we are doing that, aren't we? He comes to you three days a week when, in my opinion, he would be far better playing games.'

'Starting next term,' said Madame, 'I shall want him to have two private classes with Eduardo. There will be no charge for these. They will be my contribution to the scholarship I feel confident he will get.'

'Scholarship!' said the doctor. 'What scholarship?'

'To the Royal Ballet Senior School.'

'Royal Ballet!' the doctor gasped. 'Royal Ballet!'

'It won't be for some while yet,' said Madame. 'But if he is to get a place in the company, as I believe he can, he must start serious work this autumn.'

The doctor clung to one hope. 'It is not for me to decide. Peter must do that.'

'Quite,' Madame agreed. 'I haven't mentioned my hopes to him. Will you tell him what I have said and leave the answer to him?'

The doctor, after a short pause, nodded his head. 'OK. I won't try and influence him. I shall tell him while we are away on holiday.'

Marcia Haydée, the Brazilian dancer, with Egon Madsen in Swan Lake

CHAPTER FIFTEEN

Giselle

'Before this term finishes,' Madame said at the end of a Saturday morning class, 'there are some more ballets I want to tell you about. The first is *Giselle*. Almost all leading ballerinas hope to dance Giselle, for it is considered the great test of a dancer's talent. I am afraid though, when you hear the story, you will think it sounds pretty silly. But when you see the ballet danced it will grip you, as it has gripped all ballet lovers since it was first produced in Paris in 1841.

'The story is based on an old Slav legend. This tells of a Queen of the Wilis who has under her command hundreds of young girls, all of whom were engaged to be married but died before their weddings. Giselle is to become one of these girls. Dressed in something like a bridal dress, with flowers in her hair, condemned for ever to lure men to their deaths by forcing them to dance until they drop.

'The first act shows a little village at the time of the grape harvest. There is a great deal of mime in this act, for the audience has to be told that the gamekeeper Hilarion is in love with the young girl Giselle. Giselle, however, worships a man she calls Albrecht who is really a prince in disguise.

'The stage fills with local people and at first there is nothing but gay, joyous dancing. Then the hunt arrives at the village and Hilarion discovers Albrecht is a prince and tells Giselle. The last part of this act is what gives the ballet so great a part for a leading ballerina. The shock of knowing her Albrecht is really a prince so cannot marry her is too much for Giselle. She goes mad and in her madness tries to dance as she did when she was well. In the end, killed by grief, she dies in her mother's arms and becomes a Wilis.'

Madame looked at her watch. 'We still have a little time left, so I shall give it to a choreographer I particularly want to tell you about. Already I have told you something of her career. What I have not told you is that Ninette de Valois, as well as being a dancer and giving us a national ballet company, invented ballets which are regularly danced today. The most famous is *Job* which, when first produced,

Carlotta Grisi in Giselle

117

gave a superb part to Anton Dolin as Satan. The music was specially composed by Vaughan Williams. It is a ballet in several scenes and is based on the Bible story of the afflictions suffered by poor Job, who bears everything humbly, trusting in God. I only saw the ballet once but I have never forgotten its strange beauty.

'The next ballet Ninette de Valois choreographed was called *The Haunted Ballroom*. This is a very frightening affair. The Lord Tregennis has a haunted ballroom in his house in which each heir to the property must die in the end. The ballet shows Lord Tregennis being lured to the ballroom, where he dances himself to death. His death is seen by his young son who knows that some day he must die in the same way.

'To me,' Madame continued, 'by far Ninette de Valois's greatest ballet is *The Rake's Progress*. This ballet, with scenery and costumes by a fine artist called Rex Whistler, is based on a series of pictures by another famous artist, William Hogarth. This, in a series of scenes, shows a spendthrift sinking from riches to a most degraded end. I suppose the ballet is really more mime than dancing. But what mime! Anyway, like Eduardo, I am very fond of watching great mime.'

That was the last of Madame's talks about ballet that term. It was soon the summer holiday. Peter was going with his family to stay in Spain. Madame was going to another dancers' conference, this time in Holland. Everyone was going somewhere. 'Except me,' thought Anna. 'All I'm going to do is move to somewhere I don't want to go to. Where I'll never dance again.'

It was while they were in Spain that Peter's father talked to him about his future. They were on the beach waiting for the rest of the family to have a bathe.

'I saw that Madame of yours last term,' Peter's father said. 'She thinks you might be some good at this dancing lark. She wants you to try for a scholarship later on for the Royal Ballet School. Sounds flying a bit high to me.'

Peter thought about that.

'She won't send me to try for it if I've no chance.'

His father tried to keep the dislike he felt out of his voice. 'But would you want to be a dancer?'

Peter was not sure. 'I don't know, the thing is what else do I want to do?'

'There's tons of time to make up your mind,' his father pointed out. 'After all, you may get into a university.'

The gambling scene from The Rake's Progress

118

'I know,' Peter agreed. 'But I still won't know what I want to do. I mean, I'd loathe to be a doctor like you.'

'But do you think you want to dance?'

Peter nodded. 'I think so. Especially if I can get really good at *élévation*.'

The rest of the family were coming down the beach. Peter's father got up. 'OK. If you feel the same way when the time comes to try for a scholarship—go ahead. But I don't mind telling you I hope you change your mind.'

Anna did not even try to like her new home. She went around scowling and miserable. 'There's nothing here except miles of heather,' she wrote to Peter.

But Anna was wrong. Madame had not forgotten her, and when she returned from her conference she wrote a letter to a girl she had once taught. The result came to Anna like a magic telephone call.

'Hullo!' said a voice. 'I'm Jenny MacAndrew. Miss Deen has written to me about you. I learnt with her for some years. I hear you've moved here.'

'Yes,' Anna agreed gloomily, 'and there is nowhere to learn to dance.'

'Oh yes there is,' said Jenny. 'I have a huge kitchen and every Friday all dance lovers—and there are a lot of us—meet here and to the music of a fiddle and the bagpipes we dance reels. It's stupendous!'

'But can I get to you?' asked Anna.

'It's not far. We'll find a way. Quite often we go away to give exhibitions. We'll see how you get on; there's no reason why some day you shouldn't join the team.'

When her talk with Jenny was over Anna went back to the dining-room. Her family stared at her in amazement.

'Only one thing can have made you smile like that,' said her mother, 'you have found somewhere to dance.'

'I have,' Anna agreed. 'It sounds perfect. I'll be able to live here now.'

Illustration Acknowledgements

The author and publishers are grateful for permission to include in this book material belonging to the following:

Georgette Bordier, illustrative diagrams of ballet steps: pp. 5, 10, 11, 15, 16, 18, 19, 23, 25, 30, 38, 39, 58, 76, 80, 98, Endpapers

Aldus Books; photograph by Gerald Howson: Cover illustration

Bibliothèque de l'Arsenal, Collection Rondel, Paris: p. 49
Bibliothèque de l'Opéra, Paris, photographs by Denise Bourbonnais: pp. 29, 51, 52, 53, 54, 55, 59, 60, 72, 75, 87, 116
Bibliothèque Nationale, Paris: p. 29
Bourdelle: p. 87
British Museum: p. 20
Kim Camba: pp. 14, 42, 104–105, 121, 122–123
Alan Cunliffe: p. 90
Dance Collection, The New York Public Library at Lincoln Center, Astor, Lenox and Tilden Foundations: pp. 101, 106

Zoe Dominic: pp. 47, 88–89, 93, 95, 108–109, 119
EMI Filmproductions Ltd., London: pp. 67, 68, 69, 85
Gyula Hincz: p. 71
Valentine Hugo: p. 75
Philip Ingram: p. 102
Albert Kahn, photos from *Days with Ulanova,* published by Simon & Schuster,
    New York and William Collins Sons & Co., London: pp. 6, 17, 35, 44–45, 79, 83
Musée du Louvre, Paris, photographie Giraudon: pp. 56–57
Roy Round: pp. 31, 97, 112, 115
Society for Cultural Relations with the USSR, London: p. 27
Janine Stanlowa, Académie de Danse de Neuilly, photographs of Patricia Stanlowa:
    p. 24
H. Vizetelly: p. 64
Richard Ziegler, from *The New Ballet: Kurt Jooss and his Work* by A. V. Coton,
    published by Dennis Dobson: p. 124

Text Consultant Maria Fay
Illustration Research Julia Simonne

*Curtain call at a performance in
the Paris Opera*

p. 16

p. 80

1

2

3

p. 23

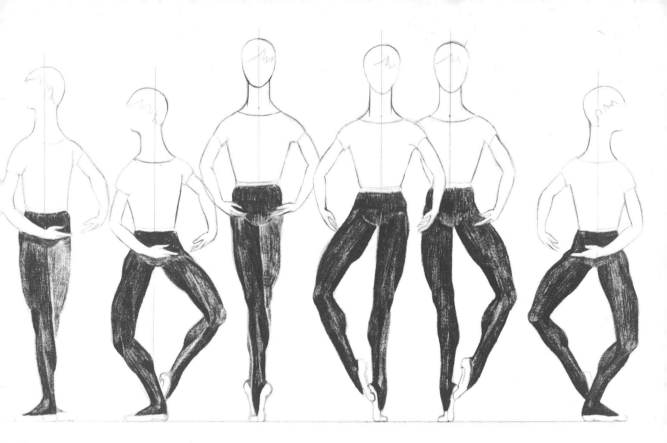

p. 38

A

C

pp. 24–25